Advance Praise for *Mystical Perelandra*

In *Mystical Perelandra*, Como draws us into the mysterious heart of the reader's experience, living within rather than merely analyzing Lewis' literary vision. The result is alchemical, poetic, and mercurial, a narrative spiritual theology where we imbibe the transcendent nature of Ransom's planetary journey through Como's imaginative, sacramental, life-integrated, mystical experience as a reader. And we are all the richer for his efforts. Como's reflections on *Perelandra* transport us, like Ransom, to a world of myth and meaning much greater than a book.

> Brenton Dickieson, author of the popular blog APilgrimInNarnia.com and Lecturer of Literature at several universities

With this unique blending of literary analysis and personal reminiscence, Como holds up *Perelandra* like a jewel, examining its many facets and explaining what makes it sparkle.

> David Downing, author of *Into the Region of Awe: Mysticism in C.S. Lewis* and Co-Director of the Marian E. Wade Center.

There are few living lovers of Lewis who know the great man's works better than James Como. This being so, anything he writes on Lewis is worth reading. His latest book contends that the art of rhetoric and the art of storytelling meet sublimely in *Perelandra*.

> Joseph Pearce, author of *Further Up and Further In: Understanding Narnia*

Mystical Perelanda is a love letter to C.S. Lewis's many and varied books, and the wonders and insights they generate, focusing on Lewis's science-fiction story, *Perelandra*. James Como presents to us the nature of the depth, imagination, and rhetorical strength of Lewis's writing.

> Colin Duriez, author of *C.S. Lewis: A Biography of Friendship*

Dr. James Como's facility to draw his readers into the multidimensional universe of Perelandra is uniquely special for an Eastern European reader with limited knowledge and understanding of the cosmology of Western Christendom, let alone of C. S. Lewis's worlds and his "intensely personal mysticism." This is not only an invitation but a brilliant and gentle guidance by Dr. Como into what he sees – more fully than in any other of Lewis's books – as Lewis intertwining "his intellectual and imaginative powers as well as the breadth and depth of the man himself."

> Dr. Denise Vasiliu, Iasi, Romania
> Founder of *The C. S. Lewis & Kindred Spirits Society for Central and Eastern Europe* and *CEO Agora Christi Center for Christian Studies and Apologetics*

Mystical Perelandra:
My Lifelong Reading of C. S. Lewis and His Favorite Book

© James Como 2022

Winged Lion Press
Hamden, CT

cover photo of Mount Kazbek, Kazbegi, Georgia by Iman Gozal

WINGED LION PRESS

ISBN 13   978-1-935688-29-7

to the members of the
New York C. S. Lewis Society,
past and present, with us and gone home

Table of Contents

Preface

This book ponders an ongoing engagement with C. S. Lewis, more particularly with his *Perelandra*, his favorite book and, for reasons I will explore, stands out from his other books monumentally. During my decades of reading him, and of writing and speaking about him, I have learned that, somehow, every one of his books stands out from the rest. In fact in many cases a Lewis book – for example, *The Screwtape Letters* as psycho-theological satire, *The Chronicles of Narnia* as fairy tale – represents a classic, or nearly so, of its type.

However, I've also realized that no single one of Lewis's books – some fifty, depending on how one counts, together constituting an astonishing array of stories (several types), essays, studies, sermons, lectures, reviews, letters, and poems long and short, of and on literary history, criticism and theory (his profession), cultural commentary (his vexations), and religious thought, devotion, exploration and inspiration (his vocation) – no single book intertwines his intellectual and imaginative powers as well as the breadth and depth of the man himself more fully than does *Perelandra*.

It is nothing less than a mini-*summa*: of the cosmology and mythology of Western Christendom, of spiritual theology (that is, of spiritual formation), and – especially – of an intensely personal mysticism, a side of Lewis insufficiently explored or appreciated. In short, *Perelandra* is an effusion.

In that regard I invite even the experienced Lewis reader to see *Perelandra*, and Lewis himself, in a fresh light, the skeptical reader to think twice, and the new reader . . . well, the new reader, I trust, will come to see that what Lewis said of his beloved Edmund Spenser is true of himself: his branches reach to Heaven, his roots to Hell, and "to read him is to grow in mental health."

This mystical Lewis was providentially sent, I believe, to live out his 'dialectic' and to provide for the rest of us who are stranded that "message in a bottle" that Walker Percy, novelist and existential philosopher, has described. In short, the Father wrought His apostle, the Spirit dispatched him, the Son, the Word Himself, lent to him expression.

That view, a long-emerging epiphany, is a triple helix consisting of a book, an author (immeasurably beyond a 'favorite'), and a reader, and it leads to another view. Lewis's significance does not lie primarily in his many books continuously in print, nor in the number of translations of those, nor in sales or movies or cultural references or even in the prodigious number of books about him and his work. It lies in his habitation in the minds, hearts, and spirits of millions upon millions of readers: there is his presence and influence, that of an authentic apostle whose spiritual engagements are a gift to us all.

Thus this short book is *not* an argument, treatise or monograph. It is not 'academic', and I trust the slight scholarly apparatus will invite many more readers than it offends. (I recall that Lewis's *Surprised by Joy* has neither notes nor bibliography.) Here I have little interest in, say, the chronology of Lewis's conversion, or in the quotidian details of his life, as important as those brush strokes are in enriching the portrait of an author whose knowing and trustworthy voice rises from the page. Still, along the way I cite sources, and the Bibliography will guide anyone interested to particular instances of those. (The mystic writers whom I cite and list separately in the Bibliography are easily found online or as e-books.)

My method is straightforward, following Lewis first (chapters one and two), then Lewis's and our hero Ransom's story (chapters three and four), and finally Ransom's and the reader's apotheosis (chapters five and six). But Lewis's own structure and narrative method in *Perelandra* display considerable technique. Moreover, his style is variously iridescent, crisp, propulsive and (literally) awesome. And how not? As I've argued over and again Lewis was a rhetorical master and knew it, no matter his distrust of the art.

As for characters, *Perelandra* has few, but a dispositive one is the setting, the planet itself. Preternatural or supernatural, or dynamically natural (particularly with respect to human psychology), it occasions an intense hyper-realism. Even the unbelieving reader swims the sea, thrills to the storm, balances on a floating island, is startled and charmed by strange, benign creatures, doubts himself before fighting an enemy hand-to-hand, exhaustedly struggles upwards in a dark and forbidding cave, and finally stands at the mountain top, beholding an unfallen world from its peak. And all of this under a close, domed sky of varying colors.

It is the sort of place that a myth requires, not merely different, as an open meadow is for a city child, but a different kind of different, as the Amazon differs from Broadway.

Since a literary object is always itself, a reader's engagement with it must be on *its* terms. If a reader has some need to convert the literary object into a sociological, political, or ideological tract no matter its nature (its own quiddity) – like the viewer of a nude marble figure responding only in carnal terms – then that reader is miserably mistaken; he is reading himself. Genuine literary reading is an immersion that goes beyond a call to action or the information on a cereal box. In its mythic dimension, *Perelandra* is that – and at the same time *meta*-literary, above and beyond, and so it requires several immersions.

Long have I noted a sub-genre of literary criticism, the sort that would settle a score. More than a few authors would take Lewis down; not take him on – that is old news, and legitimate – but do him in. The zealot Philip Pullman is one sort of those. Others, though, who having once been beguiled and now are embarrassed, would "see through" their early enthrallment. This book is the opposite, an answer: my reading would vindicate my enthrallment. And so, to those grouches, my thanks.

Deeper gratitude goes to others. There is much wisdom in many books on Lewis and his works, but one in particular, *Into the Region of Awe* by David Downing, points True North. Then there are particular friends to whom I owe much. Dennis Beets, of the Memphis C. S. Lewis Society, led me into a thematic byway that became a highway, and the encouragement of New York C. S. Lewis Society friends Dr. Clara Sarrocco and Fr. John Morrison, who read a first draft, provided some lift to my labor.

As a look back and along, as Lewis would say, this book is a coda. As I've suggested, I've come to see that his experience, thought, and the influences upon him are epitomized by this great book, often appreciated but not framed accurately or, better, not fully *celebrated* for what it is. What to say then, and how?

When I first thought to write this book, I conceived of it as a conversation intended to invite impressions, arguments, recollections, and opinions of fellow sojourners. That would be a multi-volume My Life With *or* a very short book.

For example, I remember my Lewis Firsts: I was swaying along on a New York subway train as I read *An Experiment in Criticism*; I was taken out of myself when, upon entering the home of Jack and Elaine Boise on Staten Island for the first meeting of the New York C. S. Lewis Society (1969), the assembled company rose as one to greet Alexandra and me; my excitement in 1969 at being locked in the shelved cage that was the Lewis Collection at Wheaton College, to be released from which one had to rattle the gate to beckon Mrs. Cording; our first meeting with Walter Hooper, then resident at Keble College as he looked after the recently-widowed Kay Farrer. (He quickly became "Uncle" Walter to young James and Helen Alexandra and would ask me along to visit this or that publisher to vouch for Lewis's growing popularity, sometimes asking for editorial advice.)

I remember the place of certain passages on the page (and I am far from alone in *that*). Vividly do I recall Alexandra giving me the first Lewis book I would own, *Christian Reflections*, and my father handing me a second-hand copy of *The Allegory of Love* that he had gone well out of his way to find. My children, too, were along for the journey, often interested, always supportive.

At a younger age I suppose I would have chosen that long form and been far less confessional than I am here, and yet for all its length it would have been half a book.

CHAPTER I

The Tongue is Also a Fire
"words, words, words"

Nearly at the very center of his writing career, with twenty years behind him and twenty to go until his death in 1963, C. S. Lewis published *Perelandra*, itself the centerpiece of a trilogy, its neighbors being *Out of the Silent Planet* (1938) and *That Hideous Strength* (1945). Together these came to be known as the Ransom, or Space, Trilogy, a re-mythologizing of an old cosmic model and Creation story. Over my decades of reading that mid-career middle book I have come to see it as the apogee of Lewis's dedicated apologetic project, maybe beyond his own intent.

I will try to explain, but first this: *The Screwtape Letters* (1942), coming mid-stream, and especially *The Chronicles of Narnia* (1950-56), along with everything else that Lewis wrote before and after, either led up to the impact that *Perelandra* continues to have on me or broadened and deepened it, each with its special key of psycho-spiritual revelation. Each – from poem to poem cycle to essay to book – is incomparable (though *The Chronicles* remain apart), and each moves the ready reader up toward the eschaton, the edge of eternity; that is, closer to the peak achieved by *Perelandra*.

Till We have Faces is one of five books that, in one way or another, portray Lewis's own spiritual struggles, which seem to be everyone's. Most important, though, is this particular feature of his soul-searching: words are not enough – in fact, may be too much. Consider the New Testament letter of St. James, who warns preachers and teachers to take great care in how they speak, for "the tongue is also a fire" and so they will be held to a higher standard than most. Lewis, of course, knew St. James's admonition and *was* careful, even though he wrote so much it seems he could not help himself, which he could not. By both nature and nurture he was a rhetorical machine.

Not that he did *not* know the danger of words. Always suspicious of rhetoric as a discipline (known as the Queen of the Arts in his field, the Middle Ages) and disgusted by its excesses (though treating it fairly in his professional work), he . . . worried. In a poem unpublished during his lifetime he prays, referring to his many books and the fame they brought, that God would "take from me all my trumpery[!] lest I die." In *The Silver Chair*, one of the *Chronicles of Narnia*, he brings a persuasive but evil speech to an end by a heroic act of self-sacrifice: Puddleglum the marsh-wiggle stamps on a burning fire with his naked foot. And, as we shall see, on the planet Perelandra a debate ends – our hero, Elwin Ransom, is losing – with Ransom landing a straight left hand to his adversary's chin. And then there is Orual, who must die in order for her to *stop*. A personal favorite is the young man's abrupt exhortation to the angel in *The Great Divorce*. He has been wheedling until he begs the angel to *act*, now, *right now*. Action, Lewis knew, is the important theological step in spiritual formation.

So Lewis certainly did know that an over-indulgence

in words, or an over-dependence upon them, was ultimately a losing game. In fact, at one point in his life, in the late forties, his despair was such that he felt utterly depleted, with nothing left to say – *and was thankful* if such silence would help combat the creeping sin of pride that fame was inciting. So words, to use a chess metaphor, are at best the opening. The middle game is a struggle, that is, *strife*, especially one that may very well achieve an affirmative moral reckoning or, maybe, permit or even invite something much more: a supra-real vision, the actual end game. Not easily expressed in words, that. Certainly many have tried, very few successfully.

Those few we know as mystics. I (not alone) take Lewis to be among them, *Perelandra* his fully-formed Vision. That is why, as such, it represents the pinnacle of Lewis's Christian apologetic project.

That career began in the early thirties with his tightly-wrought, intellectually complex allegory *Pilgrim's Regress*, written at high heat in two weeks. His writing *career* (not his writing, which began in early childhood: he was a prodigy) had begun in 1919 with the publication of *Spirits in Bondage*, a cycle of poems, when he was still a dozen years away from becoming a Christian. Gestation takes time. How much time?

As a young child he experienced a stab of longing, a pleasurable desire that seemed a message, almost a promise. He would call it Joy (or Sehnsucht). This experience would happen many times, unexpectedly – it could not be beckoned. (Norse mythology was a reliable portal.) In a neglected essay called 'Hedonics', a philosophy of Joy, he writes of traveling by train to Oxford from London.

As he ponders the working class 'suburbs', much scorned by sophisticates of the big city, he feels a rising pleasure as he passes the 'vales', 'woods' and 'parks' – an invitation to happiness "with all the caress of a half-remembered piece of music," like "an invitation to Eden." He accepts the "tingling" invitation, passing into a state "which can be described only as joy." I wonder: is this what he means?

> Into my heart an air that kills
> From yon far country blows:
> What are those blue remembered hills,
> What spires, what farms are those?
> That is the land of lost content,
> I see it shining plain, the happy highways where
> I went and cannot come again.

I ask because it affects me deeply. It is not Lewis, of course, but the unlikely A.E. Housman, from his *A Shropshire Lad*.

My point is that, although Lewis had no monopoly on the phenomenon, he wondered more than most and as much as the few over its source. As he would later say, God would not have made thirst had he not made a drink to satisfy it. Eventually his belief settled on this: the satisfaction of such a longing here could lie only in Christ and, later, in Heaven, our true home.

Joy, *Spirits in Bondage*, then *Dymer*, more crypto-autobiography in the form of an epic verse poem (the eponymous hero escaping from totalitarian bondage – "Of course I'm not Dymer," he would write), then a conversion to Christianity (more a process than an event: more to follow), all leading to the end of the beginning of the apologist Lewis whom most of the world has come to know, *Pilgrim's Regress*.

That is about (no surprise here) a hero escaping, lured by a longing, a desire to arrive at the origin of his painful yet sweet desire. He encounters all sorts of obstacles (menaces, delights, distractions), but also meets providential figures who advise him truly. Finally he arrives to his destination, which is where he began. (Chesterton readers – Lewis was a devoted one – will recognize the trope.) Thus do we have Lewis thinking, feeling, and imagining his way through the minefield that is a culture of unbelief (including Oxford University, where by now he is a Fellow). He is a fugitive, as he put it "behind enemy lines" no less.

In addition to Joy and Escape, however, there is another noteworthy motif, and that is the desire for a Little End Room, a place of solitude of the sort he had in the large family home during his childhood. In fact, when he finally has his own home (The Kilns, in Headington Quarry, Oxford), he would set up a simulacrum of a Little End Room for reading and writing. (Such a snug place appears in his fictions.)

So far I have passed over the many other Lewises living alongside the pilgrim: the adolescent snob, the impatient son and brother, the lover of friends and of friendship, the great walker and talker, the intellectual who could devour books and command ideas, the writer and teacher and joiner of literary groups, the combat veteran – and the sensualist. In addition to a roiling Unknown Self (his upbringing was not, as he claimed, "nominally Christian" and Joy was ever at work) his outer, official, self, was living a double life, as student and householder (of which his father, who was generous in his intellectual and financial support, must know nothing).

His liaison with a Mrs. Moore (the mother of a slain wartime buddy: he and she, with her daughter and his brother Warnie, together would buy The Kilns) – that liaison lasted until her death at age seventy-nine in 1951. She was twice his age. There is a back-story here, of course, told often enough, relevant only because it touches upon his horror-filled military service (he carried shrapnel painfully his entire life) in the trenches of World War One.

But the story is mostly a ruse: he was somehow besotted with the woman. Why? In part because his mother had died just before his tenth birthday. This I know to be an event that one may come to terms with but, no, does *not* "get over." Mrs. Moore was motherly. But also, during part of his twenties, Lewis was erotically loosely-bridled: there was some sort of sexual involvement with Mrs. Moore's which, to her bitter consternation, ended with Lewis's approach to Christianity as the decade sped on.

None of that, though, is central to the portrait I am drawing: that of a Joy-addled fugitive seeking seclusion, for that is the man who ascends to the height of his achievement as a Christian thinker, writer and seer – that mystic visionary – and takes the reader with him.

Which brings us to his conversion, and here I am something of a contrarian. My belief is that C. S. Lewis was not converted, at least not as he claimed, because he had been (albeit unbeknownst to himself: there is the Unknown Self) a sort of fellow traveler all along. He tells us in his autobiography *Surprised by Joy* that the books he liked most were by Christians, and even *Spirits in Bondage* – written presumably while he was that "blaspheming atheist," as he called himself – displays a theistic pre-disposition, as does *Dymer* (in which a young man escaping from a totalitarian state begets a monster who, after killing Dymer, becomes a god). Thus his older brother and closest friend, Warren, could honestly say that what felt to the younger man like a conversion was in fact a *recovery* from "a long mental illness." Which is why Lewis did an unsurprisingly weak job of explaining his change. It's not that he's all over the place but simply that there are so *many* places.

In *Surprised by Joy*, published in the early fifties twenty-plus years after the fact, Lewis at first uses 'chose' for his experience on that famous bus ride back to Headington from Oxford when he accepts an offer to pass through a mental door into belief. But then he immediately calls that word into doubt: "I say, 'I chose,' yet it did not really seem possible to do the opposite. . . ." His description of his ride to the Whipsnade Zoo (to see Bultitude the bear) in the sidecar of Warren's motorcycle is even less helpful: when he left home he did not believe Jesus was God incarnate, when he got there he did, but don't ask *him* why that happened: he cannot say.

The places accumulate. A late-night walk in the woods with friends about myth (which Lewis found compelling), emphasizing that a myth could *also* be fact (as is the Incarnation), though pivotal in his conversion, was necessary but impossibly insufficient, as is his literary critical judgment that the portrayal of Jesus in the Gospels is reliable reportage. That is, the writers witnessed Jesus, recorded what they witnessed, and so provide a credible view of the charismatic, highly articulated Figure, making for the famous trilemma that the Figure was either crazy, demonic, or, yes, God (leaving no space for a mere mortal, even a highly ethical, visionary, mortal).

In *Mere Christianity* we begin with the existence of *Natural Law* ("We have all heard people quarrelling" is the famous opening sentence) that eventually leads to conviction. In several writings we learn that *Reason* is the best evidence against Materialism, leading to the inevitable, particularly in the terrifically suggestive and moving peroration of *Miracles* (about which more later on). In "The Seeing Eye" he points to his *conscience* as the *agent provocateur* that begins his submission. (The "long-evaded encounter happened at a time when I was making a serious effort to obey my conscience.") And yet Law, Reason, and Conscience would have company.

In *Surprised by Joy* Lewis offers a *philosophical* map (emphasizing Bishop Berkeley's Idealism, which he allows he's never gotten over: the world as an idea in the mind of God) that leads towards, *but does not catalyze*, the great epiphany. Of course, we know that *Joy* – the unquenchable longing – was also central to the process; he always, and in the unlikeliest of places, brings forth the Hope that is conveyed by that *Sehnsucht*, for example in *The Problem of Pain*, the last chapter of which is titled 'Heaven'. Moreover, that first Christian book, the explosion that is *Pilgrim's Regress*, is about little else, playing out the "dialectic of desire" by way of which he worked to find his way home.

In short, though he had his reasons to 'convert', he also had his motives, namely this constellation of several *places*. In any given place his progressions are *reasonable*, sure, *but finally motivational*. And as with his apologetic project, just so with his recovery: inferential, illative, and ultimately existential. (An uncompelled decision arising out of a concrete psychological or spiritual experience, or a gathering of experiences, is at the center of an existential moment.) In short, *Lewis was his own apologetic project*, one he would spend a lifetime sharing with the rest of us.

In *A Philosophical Walking Tour with C. S. Lewis (Why It Did Not Include Rome)* Stewart Goetz has shown that Lewis's process was "mental-to-mental causation" (*so* many places); then, relying upon *Miracles*, he reminds us that such a process is "apprehended, grasped . . . [and] becomes part of a reasoning (inferential) process," producing beliefs. But how so? An answer, I think, lies with the great psychologist of belief, the Blessed Cardinal John Henry Newman and his *An Essay in the Aid of a Grammar of Assent*.

It took Newman twenty years to write his *Grammar* (1870), exploring such concepts as choice, reason (including logic), intuition, apprehension (a mental snatching), understanding, inference, and this ever-compelling 'illative sense'. These are central to any discussion of Newman's thinking on intellectual and psychological affirmation, and so, too-briefly, I adumbrate them here, suggesting that *Lewis's conversion followed Newman's own roadmap.*

Apprehension Newman says, is possible without understanding and can lead to belief. *Inference*, on the other hand, can be conditional. If 'informal' it is an accumulation of "converging . . . possibilities." Then, a simple, integrated process "grasps antecedent conditions of the conclusion instantaneously." The *illative* sense (as the root suggests) gets us "into" something," moves us along, as, for example, if one is seated high on a bus, or in a sidecar on the way to a zoo.

Newman compares it to other senses, like common sense, a movement across a gap: with it one recognizes "converging probabilities." Thus, "when we make the mental act expressed by 'I know', we sum up the whole reflex of judgments which might . . . exercise a critical function."

At that point one does what Lewis did. After describing his "not-choice" on the bus in *Surprised by Joy*, he writes, "enough had been thought, and said . . ." Then, exactly like many of his characters (e.g. Puddleglum, Ransom, Orual), he stops rhetorizing and acts, that is, he submits (required in spiritual theology, but more on this later).

Newman writes this about such a convert: "They come, not so much to lose what they have, but to gain what they have not; and in order that, by means of what they have, more may be given to them." The apparent contradictions of the decision by philosophy or science do not matter, he argues, for those are "reasoned in different mediums." We know to hold firm to what "heaven dictates."

Just as Lewis noted, among those *diktats* is Conscience. Newman quotes St. Thomas, "Conscience is the practical judgment or dictate of reason, by which we judge what *hic et nunc* [here and now] is to be done as being good, or to be avoided as evil." Those words are not in the *Grammar*, but this is: "I assume, then, that Conscience has a legitimate place among our mental acts. . . . [I]n this special feeling, which follows on the commission of what we call right or wrong, lie the materials for the real apprehension of a Divine Sovereign and Judge."

That Lewis merely mentions (early in his correspondence) but does not amply engage a thinker of Newman's stature is anomalous. (Though I've heard of, I've never seen, Lewis's annotated copy of the *Grammar*.) Perhaps it was Newman's conversion to Catholicism; Lewis would have none of that subject, not even in conversation with the dead, at least not publicly. In the event, there is small chance that he was not influenced by his great predecessor.

I first saw the name C. S. Lewis in 1965 in the article "The Re-Birth of Christ" by Jeffrey Hart, in *National Review* magazine. I could not believe that a commanding, prestigious literary academic could – with *argument* – rout the unbelieving enemy *in its own lair*. I would learn more. Yet when I first encountered *Perelandra*, in 1967, I knew nothing of the Lewis I've written about so far.

The trove of primary and secondary material, as well as much biographical information, was yet to come. (For example, the general reading public, at least in America, did not know that he had been married.) But Lewis's popularity was rising; that is, re-rising. After The Second World War and during the fifties his reputation peaked, his image appearing on the cover of *Time* magazine (owing largely to *The Screwtape Letters*). Then after his death his popularity declined.

But for the initiative, foresight and labor of two men, Clyde Kilby, who at Wheaton College founded the Lewis Collection which would become the Wade Center, and Walter Hooper, an American who had met Lewis, briefly acted as his secretary, and then, moving to Oxford, became one of his executors and the editor of his posthumous works – but for these two men Lewis's reputation would not have recovered, at least not as richly as it has nor as quickly.

Reading Lewis, reading, thinking and talking *about*

17

Lewis, was like breathing pure oxygen, or rather like emerging from some depth into fresh air: Lewis was *my* discovery. So I was astonished to learn that there were many others like me and always had been. (Sometimes one discovers someone and really thinks that he has *discovered* that someone.) Just so did fourteen discoverers begin the New York C. S. Lewis Society in 1969, the oldest and largest of such groups and still going strong. Good people, who over the years have come and gone but who mostly have come and stayed (and sometimes have been sneeringly, and falsely, derided as "cultists"), have been collective lab partners and would change my life, not least because among them are my dearest friends.

Shortly after that founding I traveled to Oxford and met Walter Hooper, who became a lifelong friend to me, my wife, and my family; rather like an older brother, as I described him in memoriam on the occasion of his death in 2021 at age eighty-nine. As Lewis puts it, all along a secret Master of the Ceremonies has indeed been at work.

I decided to write a master's thesis on *Perelandra* (and eventually a doctoral dissertation on Lewis's rhetoric); I traveled to what was then the Lewis Collection at Wheaton College (an aisle between two library bookshelves which, with its grated door at one end and wall at the other, resembled a monk's cell: the collection consisted of two file cabinets and several shelves); I met Clyde Kilby; I traveled to Oxford (Lewis's cozy, quirky, fitting world, already quite faded forty years ago but even now, distantly, retaining great imaginative appeal); I met and became a lifelong friend of Walter's; I taught Lewis to many students who have become lifelong readers; I wrote and lectured and opined on radio and television. Who knew? The progression seems to me at once both surprising and inevitable. Like a great *magister*, Lewis enacted what the Greeks called *psychagogia*, leading me forth and enlarging my soul.

Though at the beginning I may not have known much of Lewis, I was learning something of his work: of his literary criticism (*An Experiment in Criticism* was the first book of his that I read, and it rocked me), *The Great Divorce* (a bus trip to Heaven? Oh my), *Christian Reflections* (the first posthumous essay collection, edited by Hooper and a gift to me from my wife-to-be: it taught me a very good deal about thinking), and on and on, until I arrived at *Out of the Silent Planet*. (I found *That Hideous Strength* to be an acquired taste.) When *The Chronicles of Narnia* arrived I was twenty years old and already two or three years into my Lewisian pursuit. In truth, I had no idea then how rich the path would turn out to be, but I did know that I would follow it.

The reasons, in a nutshell, are these. I have always been an argumentative person, even as a child. I wanted reasons, and if they came my way I would question them. And, my goodness, could Lewis argue! He broke down an adversary's ideas to their underlying assumptions, often unexamined and false, confronted counter- arguments, then eventually, after what his friend Owen Barfield would later call "dialectical obstetrics," nailed down his point. So the very first, and enduring attraction, was intellectual.

Then came imaginative propulsion. That began with *The Great Divorce*, combining fantasy, the psychology of sin, *and* argument. Soon I made the voyage to Malacandra, that is, Mars, in *Out of the Silent Planet*: greater fantasy, astonishing literary psychology (Lewis knew his readers' expectations and played upon those keys like a virtuoso), and – argument. But in this case there was also a design that invited participation, a puzzle to be solved, a correspondence. And so entered Myth, a story that "could have been historical fact" but, even if not, so conveyed a truth, or a collection of truths, that it was not only compelling but convincing: yes, one could say, I see how those truths hang together.

Next came holiness. *Perelandra* proved irresistible, as narrative, argument, spiritual psychology, and as *sanctifying myth*. For decades I have been re-reading it and dwelling within it, and I do not know how Lewis could have produced it except as a mystical irruption strained through his mightily equipped intellect and story-telling genius.

For me what followed *Perelandra* was no footnote, for *The Chronicles of Narnia*, "The Weight of Glory" (Lewis's central statement of Joy), "Transposition," "The World's Last Night," "Meditation in a Toolshed"(!), and so many other essays, along with *Mere Christianity, The Problem of Pain, The Screwtape Letters* (for two months I studied Lewis's manuscript in the Berg Collection of the New York Public Library), and eventually the landmark novel *Till We have Faces* (his best literary fiction, both he and I agree) – all these and more (for example, his plenitude of letters, which I first encountered in a file drawer at the Wheaton College Lewis Collection) could only deepen and broaden the avenue revealed by *Perelandra*.

Lewis may have dismissed all of what I had read as "words, words, words, led out to do battle against other words" or as "trumpery," but he was wrong. Souls were in the balance, and he had a thumb on the scale, at least on mine. Could a cradle Catholic such as I learn about his Christian faith from Lewis, who had a lingering bias against Catholicism (a bias he admitted)? I did, not least because he did not try to talk me out of that faith. I've since learned that not only have many people come to Christ because of Lewis's influence but to Rome (which, notwithstanding puzzlement and rumors to the contrary, he never did: another story).

The fourth thread of attraction was that of other worlds and the creatures that inhabit them. I had always enjoyed faerie, fantasy, and some science fiction, in comic books, in Anderson's short tales, in collections by the Brothers Grimm, in Andrew Lang's fairy books, on television and in the movies; anywhere I could find it. As a young child – three or four? – I had invented my own Other World, the Potsie Combe, with its own king, Moonie Ma Moonlight, who could play with the moon and who invited me to rise up and join him. Lewis seemed to take such a pre-disposition and such travel seriously, as though they meant something, pointed somewhere. Lewis not only took me out of this time-space continuum but out of myself, the genuine totalitarian prison.

And that takes me to the fifth thread of attraction, Lewis's subjects and his style of writing about them. C. S. Lewis was trained in, taught, and could do philosophy, but he was not a philosopher professionally, notwithstanding his *The Abolition of Man*, a fundamental defense of Natural Law. He was a penetrating religious thinker and wrote some theology, but he was no theologian, notwithstanding the exquisitely argued *Miracles*. Though a capable poet – a number of his poems are in the first rank, especially if modernist and post-modernist biases are ignored – his living nevertheless could not have lain there. So, then, exactly what *was* he?

As Lewis was teaching me much about many things, I have watched his *habits* of mind and imagination. Lewis the journalist, essayist, and critic; the philosopher and historian; the diarist, letter-writer, and teacher; and Lewis the public figure of public houses, walking tours and devoted friendships; the lover of nature and of conversation with all sorts of folk – these Lewis's have taught me *as a matter of habit* to make distinctions, to see through prejudices, to value things-as-they-are, to track down and to test the unexamined assumptions that underlie received opinion, neither taking the world for granted nor entirely trusting it, and much else: intellectual excitement.

And this next habit, too, a sixth thread of attraction. In his Preface to *Mere Christianity* he wrote, "Ever since I became a Christian I have thought that the best, perhaps the only, service I could do for my unbelieving neighbors was to explain and defend the belief that has been common to nearly all Christians at all times." His friend Austin Farrer summarized that vocation aptly in "In His Image" (in *Remembering C. S. Lewis*):

> There are frontiersman and frontiersman, of course. There is what one might call the Munich school, who will always sell the pass. . . . They are too busy learning from their enemies to do much in defense of their friends. The typical apologist is a man whose every dyke is his last ditch. He will carry the war into the enemy's country; he will not yield an inch of his own.

In short, he was brave, and I came to love him for that.

But Farrer also accounts for his friend's success, a

spiritual and mental vastness that he placed in the service of his apostolic vocation:

> He had more actuality of soul than the common breed of men. He took in more, he felt more, he remembered more, he invented more. . . . [He] records an intense awareness . . . a taking of the world into his heart, which must amaze those whose years have offered them a processional frieze in several tints of grey. . . . His ecstasies and miseries were the tokens of a capacity for experience beyond our scope.

There is the man who has welcomed his readers' company and my companionship for nearly sixty years, and who has brought us to that rim of the eschaton. But before that he taught me this. In "Is Theology Poetry?" he writes, "I believe in Christianity as I believe that the Sun has risen, not only because I see it, but because by it I see everything else," a monumental, life-changing lesson, applicable to things in the world both large and small, every day, in its simile so unmistakably clear – and yet so casually, so firmly posited: a matter of simple fact. And that is the simple fact that drove me to 2Cor 4:16-18:

> Therefore, we are not discouraged; rather, although our outer self is wasting away, our inner self is being renewed day by day. For this momentary light affliction is producing for us an eternal *weight of glory* beyond all comparison, as we look not to what is seen but to what is unseen; for what is seen is transitory, but what is unseen is eternal.

Still, before landing in Perelandra we should survey those lower worlds, our fraught landscapes: the *Self*, *Culture*, the *Space-Time Continuum*. If we are diligent, and pay attention, and follow along, we will make it through. I've noted that the fugitive journey was his mission from very near the beginning of his writing life, as a young child. In *Dymer* (1926, his first long narrative poem) he is longing:

> Too often have I sat alone
> When the wet night falls heavily,
> And fretting winds around me moan,
> And homeless longing vexes me
> For lore that I will never know,
> And visions none can hope to see,
> Till brooding works upon me so
> A childish fear steals over me.

And he is *escaping* from the Perfect City, "for we have seen the glory, we have seen." At this point he still regards himself as an atheist! Nearly thirty years later he writes "The Prudent Jailer": "Yes. Looking at bars / and chains, we think of files."

First, then, we have the *Self,* and this question: How is the *Self* an *other* world, given that we speak as though we possess it, are coterminous with it, and that we know we cannot inhabit any other self except by imagination in art or by psychosis? We (I) are (am) that world. As with all worlds, some of it we know, much of it we do not. Some of it we display, some we hide. It is the most satisfying, treacherous and ambivalent challenge, the most elusive ambiguity in all His creation. It is what we both contemplate and enjoy (to use the Lewisian dichotomy: look *at* from the outside, experience *along* from the inside).

About it Lewis writes, "now, the self can be regarded in two ways. On the one hand, it is God's creature, an occasion of love and rejoicing; now, indeed hateful in condition, but to be pitied and healed" ("Two Ways with the Self"). However

(Lewis continues), *I* and *me* often make irrational demands for preference. "This claim is to be not only hated, but simply killed" – paying less attention to it *except* as a repairman pays attention to a broken dishwasher. "One form of rationing we ought to impose on ourselves," Lewis writes in "The Trouble With X": to "abstain from all thinking about other people's faults. . . . In each of us," he concludes, "there is something growing up which will of itself *be Hell* unless it is nipped in the bud."

Moreover, we will gain the Self that is intended for us in Heaven. In *Mere Christianity*, near the very end (IV.11 ["New Men"]), we read, "give up your self, and you will find your real self. . . . Look for yourself, and you will find in the long run only hatred, loneliness, despair, rage, ruin and decay" – the essence of spiritual theology, his and our spiritual development.

Lewis's masterpiece of modern literature, *Till We Have Face*, is fundamentally about nothing but getting out of the Self. A number of his poems – for example, "As the Ruin Falls" and "The Apologist's Evening Prayer" – convey the same desire. Is the glorious peroration even of *An Experiment in Criticism* anything but a call to be freed from the Self? Negatively, his diary (*All My Road Before Me*) exhibits a nearly-mad self-investment, which finally he escapes.

His dispositive statement comes, of course, in *Surprised by Joy*, when he discerns the purpose of Desire: "I thus understood that in deepest solitude here is *a road right out of the self,* a commerce with something which, by refusing to identify itself with . . . any state of *our own minds,* proclaims itself sheerly objective." (My emphases)

The theme winds through the much of Lewis's work. He is never done with it. In the final chapter of *The Problem of Pain* we read, "the thing you long for summons you away from the self." Of course, he recommends other means of escape than Joy: love, literature, nature, friendship, prayer. But none can ever be permanent. Only in Heaven do we get a new name, known only to God, *and become the real Self we are meant to be.*

So there we have Lewis's – and our – escape from our smallest Other World, the 'mine' that must be laid aside. But the Self is born, not into a cave but a *Society* and a *Culture*, our second Other World, and for this one, unlike the first, Lewis has scant sympathy.

In "Willing Slaves of the Welfare State" his target might be a social policy, but more deeply his warning is directed against a philosophically collectivist cultural claim:

> Let us not be deceived by phrases about 'Man taking charge of his own destiny'. All that can really happen is that some men will take charge of the destiny of the others . . . The more completely we are planned the more powerful they will be.

That is aggressive, certainly, but slightly *less* hostile than his most belligerent anti-cultural statement, "Lilies that Fester," in which he explicitly urges "rebellion," claiming "there is no time to spare." That attack is not on culture but on its self-conscious consumption and its harmful consequences.

More radical is Lewis's treatment of culture *per se*: his *uprooting* of its claims is astonishing. He argues that the 'culture' – or, better, Culture – now seems to have achieved hegemony and demands for itself exactly the diffidence that we should never afford it. Note this . . . cheekiness . . . in nearly trivializing (is that too strong a word?) an existential threat to Western Culture in "Learning in Wartime," a sermon preached at the Church of St. Mary the Virgin on December 22, 1939:

> The war creates no absolutely new situation: it simply aggravates the permanent human situation. . . . Human culture has always had to exist under the shadow of something infinitely more important than itself. . . . I reject at once . . . that cultural activities are in their own right spiritual and meritorious.

Closer to the bone is "Christianity and Literature." There Lewis argues that a striking contrast exists between the basic principles of modern literary values and those of the New Testament: 'creative', 'spontaneous', and 'freedom' rule the former; whereas 'convention', 'rules', and 'discipleship' inform the latter: not an argument against culture *per se*, but certainly the sort of skepticism that breaks ranks.

He goes further still in "Christianity and Culture." Strictly natural orders of creation, including culture, "is held on sufferance" within a Christian, supernatural, perspective, and that the New Testament is "decidedly cold to culture." "Good taste" is not a spiritual value.

Finally (for our purposes) there is "On Living in an Atomic Age." Such an age, Lewis tells us, is no different than "an age of Viking raids, plague, or death-by-auto accident." Furthermore, all civilizations will end in oblivion and their durations will have been infinitesimal compared to the "oceans of dead time" both before and after. His commanding perspective is not only *not* cultural or *merely* counter-cultural, but *supra*-cultural – and so seems quite orthodox – if you share an eternal perspective. That is, *he helps us see culture, not as a devotional artifact but as an idol.*

Enter *The Screwtape Letters.* Consider this, from the fifth letter: "the European humans have started another of their wars. . . . But what *permanent* [my emphasis] good does it do us unless we make use of it for bringing souls to Our Father Below?" Or this, from the fifteenth letter:

> The humans live in time, but our Enemy destines them to eternity. He therefore . . . wants them to attend chiefly to two things, to eternity itself, and to that point of time which they call the Present. . . . Our business is to get them away from the eternal, and from the present. . . . far better to make them live in the future [which is] of all things the thing least like eternity.

So much for Space and Time. Could any writer – any with Lewis's consistency – provide his height and breadth of perspective? The achievement transports the reader to the outer reaches of creation – and transports us to Perelandra

CHAPTER II

Hope

mystic Lewis

On the planet Perelandra – a bounteous and beguiling Paradise of water, floating islands, multi-colored sky and Fixed Land – there dwelt a Green Lady and her King. Maledil, Maker of All Things, gave them all they could want, but He forbade them ever to remain on the Fixed Land during the night. The Green Lady and the King returned Maleldil's love and obeyed Him. Then it happened that the Lady and the King became separated. At that time the Dark Power of Earth, enemy of Maleldil and all of His creatures, came to the Lady in the form of a human, who welcomed the Dark Power into himself. He tried to persuade her to disobey Maleldil, and he might have succeeded had not Ransom, one of Maleldil's loyal servants from Earth, intervened. In spite of the mortal danger to himself and at the cost of great suffering, he fought the Dark Power and drove him into the Deep. After grotesque suffering and horror in the midst of terrifying darkness, Ransom found himself close to the dome of the Perelandran sky, high on the fixed land and approaching the peak of its mountain. There, with the wound he received during his struggles healing but never closing, he rested for one year. Then he witnessed the Great Dance of creation, a design where all creatures are in the Center. He conversed with the King and Queen and spoke with the *eldila* called Mars and Venus. And so it came to pass that the Green Lady and the King were raised to high glory as the Father and Mother of a New Beginning. At last Ransom was returned to Earth. What I, Lewis, tell you was told to me by Ransom.

That is how I saw the story at my very first reading and how, after re-readings and readings-about, see it still: self-contained, fully formed, ethereal, timeless, a world almost tasteable. It filled me with an awe that would exceed the awe ignited by Narnia. More important: somehow, I knew not how, *it gave me hope.*

I wrote that description, with its semi-biblical language, not long after my first reading, fifty-five years ago. Back then I was completing the course-work for my first Master's degree (in Rhetoric and Public Discourse), knew I would soon be married, and had no job prospects. (As it happened, I'd be married, as I remain, to the same woman for over fifty years and would get a teaching position that would last for forty-nine, until my retirement.) Withal, I have not gotten over *Perlandra.*

My non-Lewis reading was preponderantly academic, including literary criticism, medieval literature (that would be my second Master's degree), and – *rhetoric,* to which I had been drawn long before I discovered it as a discipline. Recreational reading was scattered, with some Golden Age science fiction, Poe, Thornton Wilder, *An American Tragedy* (for six months I *was* Clyde Griffiths), books by famous lawyers (especially *Courtroom*, by the great Samuel Leibowitz, who defended the Scottsboro boys and whom I would later meet), short stories, and – more Lewis. This blossoming in my intellect and imagination was soon interrupted a deep dive into Aristotle's *Rhetoric*. (But it's best to think of the Lewis 'interruption' as a process, not an event.)

I was a church-goer who said his prayers, the most Catholic member of my family, my belief and practice reinforced by my observant Peruvian wife-to-be. So I was more than 'nominally Catholic', or Christian, but not much more. That very personal *weltanschauung* would broaden and deepen during the next three decades, and thereafter exponentially, always in the company of a catalyzing, instructive, wonder-working C. S. Lewis and the books he led me to (especially Chesterton), no small thing, as devoted readers of Lewis well know.

What matters now, though, is that I did not realize then that Lewis was becoming a guide for me: intellectual, imaginative, spiritual. Like Lewis's – like everyone's – my Official Self was busy. Student, husband, father, teacher, friend, son, brother, the last two taking up much temporal, physical and emotional oxygen for decades: a long story that began with my mother's death when I was eight years old: all left scant space for a Little End Room. Even baseball and movie-going were compromised. Travel to Peru changed me: I was smitten and would return fifty times, eventually writing about it both academically and as a fully-credentialed foreign correspondent.

But that Official Self at the young adult stage had company, a Self marked by a roiling spiritual unrest: enter Lewis, and *Perelandra*. At first, and for a long, long time, I knew – I see it in my own pseudo-mythical description of *Perelandra* – that the book had sunk roots into my soul and imagination, which I've since learned overlap considerably. No. 'Overlap' is the wrong word. 'Interanimate' is much better, as Lewis would learn, not least from his friend Owen Barfield. Yet I attributed that influence, not to Lewis's visionary dynamism but to his – *rhetoric*: nothing 'mere' about it, ever or anywhere. The marriage – vision and word – was inevitable, made, I thought, in Heaven (perhaps literally). I would write a thesis or two about it, then later a book.

That word, 'rhetoric', I know, resonates differently with different people, and only with a minority is the resonance positive. For me the opposite has always been the case. That (especially the marriage of Lewis and rhetoric) may sound foolish to a 'civilian', or to a greater believer than I, but such is the reach of rhetorical theory, its scope and depth, that it proves itself a powerful explanatory tool.

I said in the previous chapter that Lewis was a rhetorical machine, whether he liked it or not, and I mean it. At its practice he was a *very* great genius. Through that lens did I see Lewis, and have so seen him, profitably I believe, ever since. Paradoxically, I applied the same lens to the end of *Perelandra*, only to learn that mystical vision supersedes rhetoric. Just like words generally, rhetoric is not enough.

Lewis, a one-man Argument from Design, surely, had a rhetorical temper that provided a compulsiveness and stance that could be resolved only in argument. Training, taste and talent equipped him for an academic and apologetic career, to the exclusion of nearly all others. Of course, he could not have remained an atheist, in his case rather an aberration than a settled state; so his conversion added direction, a high apologetic purpose, towards which, in the thirties, he explicitly turned his formidable will.

First, though: by *rhetoric* I mean that subset of questions and lines of inquiry deriving, first from Aristotle's definition in chapter two of Book One of his treatise, *the faculty of observing in the particular case the available means of persuasion*; and second from the Judeo-Christian tradition of apologetic, characterized (as suggested by St. Augustine in Book IV of his *De doctrina Christiana*) by God's "self-disclosure . . . in the contemporary world," concerning itself with the relationship between faith and reason. The apologist translates the Christian demand for faith. The conception that emerged from Aristotle and others is that of a series of systematic adjustments among purpose, circumstances, audiences and strategies. Those circumstances are unsettled by 'exigencies' – some imperfection marked by urgency which demands resolution by persuasion and thus occasions discourse.

There are constraints, of course, inherent to that occasion, the most restrictive being the limitations of what Aristotle called the 'judge', any audience empowered to 'mediate' the resolution. To these circumstances the apologist brings his resources, including a certain style (for the last century or so our preference has been for *an extension of natural, direct conversation*).

Finally, of over-riding importance is the nature of rhetoric as an *inherent faculty* of any human being: *an ineluctable feature of everyone's interior landscape.* In short, Aristotle could have begun his seminal *On Rhetoric* with the words, "all people by nature love to, and must, rhetorize."

Moreover, if Lewis had been around then, *he would have been Aristotle's model,* as *Oedipus Rex* was for his *Poetics.* His word choice, sentencing, and paragraph construction all build inexorably and unintrusively towards easy understanding, almost always punctuated by the perfect image. The pattern is preponderantly from the *possible* to the *plausible* to the intensely *pleasurable* to the concretely *promising,* and then, very often, to *glory.* There is in Lewis nothing, ever, of the sort of thing we find in Jonathan Edwards' great sermon, "Sinners in the hands of an Angry God":

> The bow of God's wrath is bent, and the arrow made ready on the string, and justice bends the arrow at your heart, and strains the bow, and it is nothing but the mere pleasure of God, and that of an angry God . . . that keeps the arrow one moment from being made drunk with your blood.

Thus, in many modes and at varying levels of intensity and directness, Lewis was relentlessly persuasive. He delivered only a handful of sermons, for example, but they made history. "Transposition" was delivered from the pulpit of Mansfield College, close to the house Lewis stayed in on his very first night in Oxford. "The Weight of Glory" and "Learning in War-Time" were preached to multitudes from the pulpit of The University Church of St. Mary the Virgin: Latimer, Cranmer and Ridley had been tried there, and Wesley, Keble and Newman had preached from the same pulpit. These are impressive venues.

But as impressive in their variety and modesty are the venues of some of his greatest essays. Here is a sampling: *St. Jude's Gazette*, *World Dominion*, *Electrical and Musical Industries Christian Fellowship*, *Coventry Evening Telegraph*, *Bristol Diocesan Gazette*, *The Month*, *Breakthrough*, and *St. James's Magazine*; of course there were also *The Saturday Evening Post*, *The Guardian* (small, but prominent in its day), *Time & Tide*, *Twentieth Century*, and *Spectator*. No venue was too large for his idiomatic voice nor audience too small for his concentrated attention.

And he was fearless, confronting the most difficult subjects. If Jesus was God, why did he not return, as he seems to have promised, during the lifetime of those who actually heard him? If we are promised that prayers made faithfully will be answered, why are they so frequently not? If God is loving, why does he permit so much suffering, especially of the innocent – even of the beasts, who were not morally complicit in the Fall? What explanation other than psychosis could explain "speaking in tongues"? In the absence of evidence why should we be "obstinate" in belief? How can we possibly reconcile *dogmatic* belief with the need freely to exercise our reason, presumably God-given? Why do we not see miracles? The range of work – in its content, mode, scope, style, and persistence – is unremitting, as is the intellectual robustness.

In its great array, the whole of the work speaks to a sufficient variety of tastes, intellectual ability, religious doubt, spiritual need, imaginative longing, levels of curiosity, and sheer patience with the written word sufficient to satisfy the preponderance of readers, no matter where they break in upon that work. In believing that Christ intends for us to be persons (members of His Person), Lewis uses an occasion to offer his audience recognizable facets of personality and to show them what they might become.

Having taken seriously the claim that the universe is possessed of meaning, he then provides an image of reality sufficiently coherent and authoritative to make the claim credible.

Lewis's scholarly treatments of rhetoric are both straightforward and a bit unsettled, especially because it unsettled him – as he shows in the debate on Perelandra (on which more later on). Of interest here is Lewis's attention to one Geoffrey of Vinsauf, whose *Nove Poetria* of the early thirteenth century achieved commanding influence. It is precisely the sort of rhetoric – one figure of speech after another, with prescriptions for beginning and ending – that would vex Lewis.

Notwithstanding his even-handed treatment of rhetorical history in his professional work, his notebooks offer virtually no use of *rhetoric* that is not derogatory, this in spite of Dante, who called it the 'the sweetest of all the other sciences'."

"I don't know if I'm weaker than other people," he said, "but it is a positive revelation to me how *while the speech lasts* it is impossible not to waver just a little," he wrote, after hearing a speech by Hitler (the night before he conceived the idea for *The Screwtape Letters!*). "I should be useless as a schoolmaster or a policeman. Statements which I *know* to be untrue all but convince me, at any rate for the moment, if only the man says them unflinchingly."

As I've mentioned, the only passenger on *The Great*

Divorce bus to Heaven who stays is the one who stops rhetorizing and exclaims, "damn and blast you! Go on can't you? Get it over" and presently shuts up.

Now, in Christian terms the spiritual dilemma is clear. When rhetoric and redemption meet in the self, one of them must give way, since rhetoric requires a voluble ego and redemption its death, as an antecedent to its re-birth and resurrection. Decades ago Owen Barfield (Lewis's "second friend" and solicitor) wrote to me that he did not think Lewis's rhetorical persona – his direct, conversational, and confessional familiarity – was deliberately adopted.

Rather, "the indifference to self" that came later, wrote Barfield, "may well have been responsible for his *maintaining* the persona throughout the rest of his life, as may also have been the thought of its usefulness for the purpose of argumentative Christian apology."

During his entire life, Lewis used himself as a *datum*, most spectacularly in *A Grief Observed* (the journal he kept upon the death of his wife) but also in *The Magician's Nephew, Till We Have Faces,* and *Letters to Malcolm*, masterpieces all. Always was he essentially that wary yet energetic, ambivalent yet committed, *homo rhetoricus.* And therein lies the problem, both his and mine.

The self upon which Lewis's genius of the will turned its back in his thirties is the very same self so palpably conspiring with his genius of rhetoric, the very same rhetoric that issued forth in response to his *willed commitment to a vocation* (his *action*, prescribed, let us recall, by spiritual theology for spiritual formation).

In his chapter on Pride in *Mere Christianity,* "The Great

Sin," he tells us that God is trying to make us humble for our own sake, "trying to take off a lot of silly, ugly, fancy-dress" of self-conceit that we are wearing. And then he confesses, "I wish I had got a bit further with humility myself: if I had, I could probably tell you more about the relief, the comfort, of taking the fancy-dress off – getting rid of the false self, with all its 'Look at me . . . '." That affliction would rise up strongly in the late forties, when he was thankful for the possibility of having nothing left to say.

So the rhetorical genius in Lewis must have presided uneasily, what with all its self-projection. In the private venue of lyric poetry this alarm surfaces explicitly in "As the Ruin Falls" (unpublished during his lifetime), addressed perhaps to Joy Davidman, perhaps to God:

> All this is flashy rhetoric about loving you.
> I never had a selfless thought since I was born.
> I am mercenary and self-seeking through and through:
> I want God, you, all friends, merely to serve my turn.
>
> Peace, re-assurance, pleasure, are the goals I seek
> I cannot crawl one inch outside my proper skin:
> I talk of love – a scholar's parrot may talk Greek –
> But, self-imprisoned, always end where I begin.

And what he finds particularly discomfiting, even alarming, is not only the effect of rhetoric upon his credulity but its hold upon his self, for that hold symptomizes an inability to let go of his old, needful theatrical ego. Listen to this *cri de coeur* that I referred to earlier, written late and also unpublished in his lifetime:

From all my lame defeats and oh! much more
From all the victories that I seemed to score;
From cleverness shot forth on Thy behalf
At which, while angels weep, the audience laugh;
From all my proofs of Thy divinity,
Thou, who wouldst give no sign, deliver me.

. . . .

Lord of the narrow gate and the needle's eye,
Take from me all my trumpery lest I die.

But surely Lewis was too tough on himself. In his *Religio Medici*, Sir Thomas Browne, a physician, sought to "exercise [his] faith in the difficultist point; for to credit ordinary and visible objects is not faith but persuasion" – thereby to reconcile the inquiring skepticism of a scientist with his deep and orthodox religious faith. So is there not for Lewis, along those lines, some *rhetorica religii*?

This would be an existential rhetoric, the sort of thing which St. Augustine, that keen, zealous, and professional rhetorician, approximated as he sought to celebrate "signs of divine presence within the human mind." I understand that 'existential' might seem odd applied to C. S. Lewis, who had no patience with Existentialism or with such of its avatars as Kierkegaard, whom he dismissed with exclamatory impatience.

I believe Lewis was wrong and that his rejection may have been preponderantly tonal. In his "Three Kinds of Men" (*Present Concerns*), for example, he describes those who seek pleasure, others who acknowledge a higher claim upon them, and a third who, like St. Paul, aspire "to live is Christ." The burden of proof is on the Defense to show how this taxonomy is *not* Kierkegaard's aesthetic, ethical, and religious stages, that Lewis was *not* a Knight of Faith incarnate, rejecting the Spirit of the Age to follow God whatever the price, and that Lewis did *not* live a dialectic that found selfhood not given but dependent upon reading the signs and choosing to follow them - all features inherent in the life and work of Kierkegaard, the godfather of Existentialism..

Here he is, in his own words. In "The Seeing Eye" (a late essay) he ponders the assertion that Russian astronauts have not found God in outer space and goes on to say things which, typically, seem manifestly self-evident, *after* he has said them, of course, but also said them almost peripherally. "If God created the universe, He created space-time" – so far, so obvious. But next comes the *subordinate clause*: "which is to the universe as the metre is to a poem or the key is to music." Well, of course! That *certainly is* space-time. (All along there is a familiar small, soft voice, at least in my head, whispering, "so *that's* space-time.")

Thus, Lewis continues, "to look for Him as one item within the framework which He Himself invented is nonsensical." After all, he adds, "a fish is no more, and no less, in the sea" – here he will drive the point home – "after it has swum a thousand miles than it was when it set out. . . . To some, God is discoverable everywhere; to others, nowhere. Those who do not find Him on earth are unlikely to find Him in space. . . ." He concludes, "much depends on the seeing eye," one like Lewis's own, a quintessentially existential exhortation.

In "Christianity and Literature," a paper from the thirties collected by Hooper in *Christian Reflections*, Lewis noted that "a cultured person . . . is almost compelled to be aware that reality is very odd and that the ultimate truth, whatever it may be, *must* have the characteristics of strangeness -- *must* be something that would seem remote and fantastic to the uncultured."

Elsewhere he would remind us that we must choose to be either "Man or Rabbit," either wanting and trying to know or pursuing the carrot of simple efficacy; or when considering "The Trouble with 'X' . . ." we must consider X's personhood, the charity it requires, and our membership in the same Body as X.

We are shipwrecked, as Walker Percy has put it, and await "the message in the bottle," one that a Seeing Eye discerns and which only the *homo rhetoricus* can translate for the rest of us who are stranded. In "The Message in the Bottle" Percy (whose summary of Christian existentialism is perfectly applicable to the author of *A Grief Observed*), provides a suggestive image of what a Christian rhetorician does:

> Existentialism has taught us that what man is cannot be grasped by the science of man. The case is rather that man's science is one of the things that man does, a mode of existence. *Another mode is speech* [rhetoric]. Man is not merely a higher organism responding to and controlling his environment. He is . . . that being in the world whose calling it is to find a name for Being, to give testimony to it, and to provide for it a clearing. [Emphasis added.]

And then there is Newman's Illative Sense. Could there be any more accurate a paradigm for Lewis's rhetoric? When the Man of Letters speaks with "auctoritee" on myth, metaphor, and meaning in language and in literature; or the Apologist reasons; or the preacher and romancer beckons; or the fellow fugitive reflects, wonders, confesses, and suggests – then he is speaking illatively, his "extension of natural conversation" sufficiently associative (i.e. 'illative') as to convey us across the gaps.

This is no "flashy rhetoric" or "trumpery," but a nuanced, thoughtful, committed religious thinker "speaking well" (as the Roman rhetor and teacher Quintilian has put it.)

In short, he would continue to act upon the distinction made by the psychotherapist Phillip Rieff, that "religious man was born to be saved; psychological man was born to be pleased." He would, because he knew that "evangelization," as Pope John Paul II writes in *Crossing the Threshold of Hope*, is the "encounter of the Gospel with the culture of each epoch."

Even when 'topical' (as in "On Living in an Atomic Age," for example) Lewis is timeless. Our "minds claim to be spirit," and "it is part of our spiritual law never to put survival first," so our survival "must be by honourable and merciful means," not that which "works" but that which is true – that which because of its coherence reveals meaning in the apparently meaningless – to win our assent.

The establishment of an *inter-connected wholeness* and a renewed confidence in our ability to apprehend it was the basis of Lewis's own conversion and became the basis of his existential appeal, his midwifery, and, behind Hope, his secondary appeal to me. Paul Holmer, in *C. S. Lewis: The Shape of His Faith and Thought*, writes:

> He shows us repeatedly . . . how a kind of moral certitude is finally achieved. He sends us back to

our fathers, mothers, nurses, poets, sages, and lawgivers. The dignity he ascribes to all of us is exceedingly flattering. . . . The tissue of life around us, when taken with seriousness, is already a moral order. We have to become its qualified readers. . . . The world has no single character, and it must be understood in a variety of ways. His books create, almost as Kierkegaard did, the living variety of paradigms. . . . Here the requirements are new capabilities, new capacities altogether. . . . For his works, especially the novels, have a way of creating a kind of longing for innocence, for purity, for humility, candor, and contentment. . . . Only its occasion can be created by another, and that is what Lewis's literature becomes. Wisdom has to be read off the whole shape of his thought and is not one trick within it.

In yet another poem unpublished during his lifetime, Lewis petitions for a certain sort of integration and maturity. In the last half of his sonnet "Reason," with Athene representing that faculty and Demeter the Imagination, he writes:

> Tempt not Athene. Wound not in her fertile pains
> Demeter, nor rebel against her mother-right.
> Oh who will reconcile in me both maid and mother,
> Who make in me a concord of the depth and height?
> Who make imagination's dim exploring touch
> Ever report the same as intellectual sight?
> Then could I truly say, and not deceive,
> Then wholly say, that I BELIEVE.

It is of more than passing interest that "I believe" is (as Lewis would have known) a close translation of 'Peitho', the Greek goddess of rhetoric, usually seen in the company of Aphrodite. Lewis was not the apostle from across the sea, as Walker

Percy describes him; rather, *he was one of us*, shipwrecked.

But unlike most people, he worked to make a clearing for the message and labored his life long to interpret it for all who are on the island with him. Precisely here lies the grave importance of *Perelandra*: it gets us *off* the island, not into a fantasy world but into a mythical one sharing our time and space. And its key is not rhetoric which, though catalytic, and perhaps sufficient for conviction, certainly is not sufficient for an awe beyond even hope itself.

I knew that, inevitably when I discussed rhetoric, I would carry on, and I am appreciative of any indulgence the reader has bestowed. So now a change of key. Lewis had an anarchic streak, certainly, or at least a very strong anti-collectivist disposition. At first I intuited, then recognized, that I shared this with him. The disposition was compromising in many ways: in the academy, in sport, even in social settings. I did not always and ever want to be by myself, but I realized that spectating was my default position. My wife and family, along with a small group of friends, remain sources of enormous happiness, never parties or movements.

And I learned to abide by the common mores of society, though a mother's early death is a handicap in that, as in many, respects – even given a wonderfully attentive and loving father. In such a father I had the advantage over Lewis, though he over me in not having a troubled and troublesome older brother at a young age.

The deepest separation was cultural. My peers listened to The Four Seasons, I to the Mills Brothers; they took lessons to be in a rock band, I played the accordion: that sort of thing. My Catholicism – as Christianity should be, must be – is counter-cultural. Thus does it *ex-sistare*, or 'stand out', getting us closer to Heaven.

Nothing about this hemi-demi-anarchy is mystical, and in my early readings of Lewis I knew of that state only abstractly. In fact, it has been called autistic; that is, on the famously-common 'spectrum'. In my case the label means nothing; if I were a visionary I'd know it. But in Lewis's case 'mystic' does mean something.

He corresponded with and read the famous early-twentieth-century mystic Evelyn Underhill. She writes that "the immanence of the Divine Spirit within the human soul . . . lies at the root of a mystical concept of life." She continues a bit further (this from her *Mysticism*, 1911): "the mystical consciousness has the power of lifting those who possess it to a plane of reality which no struggle, no cruelty, can disturb." Moreover, "it is a part of every man's life." If so, then mysticism makes fugitives of us all, from the Self, Society, Culture, and eventually from Space and Time. Of course, some of us know it more than others.

Her formal definition offers a stumbling block. *"Mysticism is the art of union with Reality. The mystic is a person who has attained that union in greater or less degree; or who aims at and believes in such attainment* [her italics]." No Lewis reader would claim that *Lewis* claimed such an attainment; his reticence is palpable. The reason, I believe, lies in the thinking and art of those I'll call the High Mystics, like St. Theresa of Avila and St. John of the Cross, who, like other mystics, strove for spiritual perfection by way of a contemplative life and "the prayer of the quiet." In short, Lewis was timorous, though the cat peeks out when he praises St. Francis de Sales's *The*

Introduction to a Devout and Holy Life, introducing souls to the purgative and illuminative ways, the first two stages of mystical ascent (unitive being the last). Maybe he was just *too* voluble.

In many ways Lewis gives tastes of that illumination, but often in the most unexpected places. *Miracles* (1947), for example, is his refutation of David Hume's attack on the possibility of miracles. Lewis knew Hume well, in fact wrote as an atheist (like Hume) and filled a notebook with ideas about him for use in his lectures. So in this tightly wrought theological work, Lewis methodically lays out Hume's case, which comes down to this, that there is "uniform experience" against miracles; that is, they never happened. Lewis responds matter-of factly: we know the experience against them is uniform only if we *a priori* reject all reports of them, which we can do only if we already know all reports of them are false.

In short, Hume argues in circles. Lewis's logic is inexorable, and as he draws to a close Lewis knows what may happen next, "that soft, tidal return of your habitual outlook" on the real world. "The dream is ending; as all other similar dreams have always ended. . . ." But, he continues, "God does not shake miracles into Nature at random. . . . Unless you live near a railway, you will not see trains go past your windows." Just before that he has written,

> These small and perishable bodies we now have were given to us as ponies are given to schoolboys. We must learn . . . that someday we may ride bareback, confident and rejoicing, those greater mounts, those winged shining and world-shaking horses which perhaps even now expect us with impatience, pawing and snorting in the King's stables.

We have had reason. Now followed imagination. Both are calls to hope – and that in one of the two pure theological works he ever wrote.

A second taste comes in *The Problem of Pain* (1940). His logic is looser there than in *Miracles*; he is more speculative, though still systematically. The origins of religion (the numinous: Rudolph Otto's *The Idea of the Holy* is always nearby for Lewis), and the concepts of omnipotence, free will, and The Fall are lined up. We read that pain is God's megaphone to a deaf world, and that we don't want a Father in Heaven as much as we want a Grandfather (. . . how well I've come to know what *that* means).

But as with *Miracles*, intellection is not enough. Very near the end we get a chapter on Heaven, where we read: "The thing you long for summons you away from the self. . . . There is Joy in the 'celestial' dance" – note, a *dance* – "It is Love Himself, and Good Himself, and therefore happy." (I note that Ramandu, the retired star of *The Voyage of the 'Dawn Treader'*, longs once again to tread the "celestial dance.")

Surely Lewis knew more, saw more, than he was letting on? In a letter he would write of mysticism, "there is no reasoning in it, but many would say it is an experience of the intellect – the reason resting in its enjoyment of its object." I had not yet read *Surprised by Joy*, but I was intuiting the allure of Lewis's authentic appeal. Though my first attraction to him was through his intellect, particularly his thrilling dialectical skill, the call to my spirit was not that, and to find that call at the end of those two books – such imagery should not have been in such places! – was more thrilling still.

Then I came upon his sermon "The Weight of Glory"

(1941), Lewis's definitive statement respecting Joy, and there it was.

> Do you think I am trying to weave a spell? Perhaps I am; but remember your fairy tales. Spells are used for breaking enchantments [too] . . . to wake us from the evil enchantment of worldliness . . . all the leaves of the New Testament are rustling with the rumour that it will not always be so. Some day, God willing, we shall get in . . . . there are no *ordinary* people. You have never talked to a mere mortal. Nations, cultures, arts, civilization – these are mortal, and their life is to ours as the life of a gnat. But it is immortal . . . horrors or everlasting splendors . . . [that] we joke with, marry, snub, or exploit.

With that I began to remember: the floral pattern on my mother's housedress, the late afternoon sun (more amber than yellow) shining on us as we napped, a thick stand of trees below Alexandra's and my honeymoon hotel on the island of Skiathos, the Alhambra in Granada (virtually empty on our first trip), the opening of Chaucer's General Prologue, Helprin's *Winter's Tale*, Wilder's *The Woman of Andros*, my first view of the inside of Yankee Stadium, hyper-real at night, an inside that took you outside, many places in Peru (especially on the *altiplano*) – and many more, so many calls about, or from, one Place. I could understand what Lewis means when he tells us, "joy is the serious business of Heaven."

A regular reader of Lewis knows that such calls abound in his writing, but he warns us not call for or to expect such moments. Here is "The Day With the White Mark," not published during his lifetime:

All Day I have been tossed and whirled in a preposterous

48

happiness:

Was it an elf in the blood? or a bird in the brain? or even part

Of the cloudily crested, fifty-league-long, loud up   lifted wave

Of a journeying angel's transit roaring over and through my heart?

My garden's spoiled, my holidays are cancelled, the omens harden;

The plann'd and unplanned miseries deepen; the knots draw tight.

Reason kept telling me all day my mood was out of season.

It was, too. In the dark ahead the breakers only are white.

Yet I – I could have kissed the very scullery taps. The colour of

My day was like a peacock's chest. In at each sense there stole

Ripplings and dewy sprinkles of delight that with them drew

Fine threads of memory through the vibrant thickness of the

soul.

* * * * * * * * * * * * * * *

Who knows if it will ever come again, now the day closes?

No-one can give me, or take away, that key. All depends

On the elf, the bird, or the angel. I doubt if the angel himself

Is free to choose when sudden heaven in man begins or ends.

This is Joy, what he taught me to recognize. We see this sort
of things *by way of it*: the sun that is Christianity.

When I finally arrived at Narnia, I, like millions of
others, was transported by some "journeying angel's transit,"
as when Aslan breathes on Susan and on the statues, and
when Lucy tells Aslan that it's not Narnia but him she will
miss so longingly, or when Frank the cabbie, witnessing the
creation of the new world that will be Narnia (an ambitious
piece of writing rarely matched), proclaims, "Glory be! I'd ha'
been a better man all my life if I'd known there were things
like this." Is that not what Isaiah promises (61:3)? "To grant

to those who mourn in Zion . . . the oil of gladness instead of mourning, the garment of praise instead of a faint spirit; that they may be called oaks of righteousness, the planting of the Lord, that he may be glorified."

In recalling a conversation from 1926, Lewis epitomized his apprehension of that oil: "The hardest boiled of all the atheists I ever knew," he writes, "said, 'All that [anthropological] stuff . . . about the Dying God [especially in Sir James George Frazer's *The Golden Bough*]. Rum thing. It almost looks as if it had really happened once.'" That is, the shape of the story – a god coming down among us, dying, then rising again – had a resonant allure. There is an early adumbration of a conception of Myth, which we will explore later on.

That it became fact – what Lewis learned from a late-night conversation with Tolkien and Hugo Dyson – is what he wrote of on October 25th, 1934, to the critic Paul Elmer More: "Is the Christian belief not precisely this; that the same being which is eternally . . . at the End . . . yet also, in some incomprehensible way, [is a] purposing, feeling, and finally crucified Man in a particular place and time? So that somehow or other, we have it both ways?"

In 1 Thes 5:8 we are told to "put on faith and love for a breastplate and the hope of salvation for a helmet." Rom 5:5 drives the point home: "Those sufferings bring patience, patience brings perseverance, and perseverance brings hope, and this hope is not deceptive because the love of God has been poured into our hearts by the Holy Spirit which has been given us." At the very end of the last book he saw through the press, *Letters to Malcolm, Chiefly on Prayer* Lewis writes:

> I don't say the resurrection of this body will happen
> at once. It may well be that this part of us sleeps in
> death, and the intellectual soul is sent to Lenten
> lands where he fasts in naked spirituality – a ghost-
> like and imperfectly human condition. . . . Then
> the new earth and sky [not unlike the New Narnia
> emerging at the end of *The Last Battle*], the same
> yet not the same as these, will rise in us as we have
> risen in Christ. And once again . . . the birds will
> sing and the waters flow, and lights and shadows
> move across the hills, and the faces of our friends
> laugh upon us with amazed recognition. Guesses,
> of course, only guesses. If they are not true,
> something better will be.

A vision beyond the Self, Society, Culture, Time and Space;
beyond even any Little End Room and the need for either
intellection or imagination, the home to which we would
escape: Lewis's irrupting mysticism provides us with our Oil
of Gladness. I say again, here is the kernel: millions upon
millions of individual human hearts have been ignited and
changed by him, because almost anywhere one looks into him
one finds the very linchpin of his apologetic project and our
salvation: Hope.

CHAPTER III

Storytelling
belief 'in'

Often overlooked in favor of his big effects, Lewis's narrative subtlety is such that the most innocuous detail coming in mid-paragraph can foreshadow great events. That is the case in one of my favorite, and most remarkable, openings in all literature.

Out of the Silent Planet (1938) begins with the hero Ransom continuing a long walk at dusk after a hard rain. "If he had chosen to look back . . . [he] might have uttered a malediction on the inhospitable little hotel, which, though empty, had refused him a bed." This completely uncharacteristic, almost unnatural violation of the unwritten law of English countryside hospitality is an ill omen indeed. It requires Ransom to walk another six miles before he can rest, and Where begins the adventure that will make him, through no will of his own, fear for his life, bring him to Malacandra (Mars), and show him a stunning reality, an entirely unforeseeable Otherness.

Much later, when he returned safely to Earth, "he stood in pitch-black night under torrential rain . . . [and] with every desire of his heart he embraced the smell of the field about him – a patch of his native planet where grass grew." There really is no place like home. When finally on a village street he sees that "a lighted door was open" – how different from the cold, unwelcoming beginning – and heard "voices from within and they were speaking English. . . . He . . . walked to the bar. 'A pint of bitter, please,' said Ransom." There (though there is a bit more to follow) is one of my favorite endings. Upon his return from Deep Heaven the imbalance of the beginning is corrected on the English countryside.

The consequence of the voyage, however, is that the cosmos is now vulnerable to the attack we will witness on Perelandra: the quarantine of Thulcandra (The Silent Planet, Earth) that confined our fallen oyarsa to within the orbit of our moon – the boundary, thought philosophers in the Middle Ages, beyond which lay immutability – has been breached.

In its narrative drive, Chapter One of *Perelandra* is remarkably different from that of its predecessor, though not quite its opposite. It is striking for its compelling psychological realism, its spiritual assertiveness, and for its narrative device. The first-person narrator is none other than Lewis – our tether to the world that we, the readers, know, an unarguably actual world – and he has a Hell of a time getting to the cottage to meet Ransom.

Once he is at the cottage he converses with his friend, who is bound for a long journey back into Deep Heaven. Would he, Lewis, come back in about one year? He would be summoned. And by all means bring a doctor with you, our friend Humphrey (that is the real life 'Humphrey' Havard, Lewis's actual physician, also known as the "U.Q." or Useless Quack).

Of course Lewis agrees, and off goes Ransom in a translucent capsule to be transported by an Oyarsa, perhaps the one Ransom has already met on Malacandra and whom Lewis had heard and seen as a rod of light. (Here I noticed, and now note, the complete and satisfying absence of actual rocketry.) Then, *before the chapter ends*, the year has gone by, Lewis and the doctor have shown up, and Ransom has returned. Thus the adventure that follows is all told as a flashback: Ransom recounting his adventure.

I was beguiled. Usually we must wait to know if our hero makes it through; here, by the end of the second chapter, we *know* he has. So the question posed immediately is: made it through *what*? Even if one had not read *Out of the Silent Planet*, the reader has already been introduced to evil spirits and eldila, the angelic creatures that populate the cosmos to serve Maleldil, the creator of it all. So my question to Lewis, that is, Lewis the author, and to myself, because by now he and I are shoulder-to-shoulder, is: What awaits me in Chapter Two?

Very early in my first reading I marveled at Lewis's narrative audacity. His hero may, or may not, recall all aspects of his adventure (who would, given *that* adventure?), including his responses (emotional and otherwise) to its variations; his doubts and physical reservations may give him (as they do John in *Pilgrim's Regress*) momentary pause, but since his presence on Perelandra is no accident he learns that though not alone he is, in his trials, on his own – which mattered greatly to me, and still does.

I already trust the utterly unposturing, practical, resolute Ransom. He is recognizably not a superhero, he knows he must be dutiful and dislikes the idea, has little understanding of his purpose but knows enough to know that understanding, in this case, is a luxury. In short, he was the young me. (I refer to a roiling domestic mess.) As the purpose becomes clear to Ransom he *is* daunted. *But what does he do next?* Or, rather, what does C. S. Lewis do next?

Sanford Schwartz has written a learned book, *C. S. Lewis on the Final Frontier*, where he notes a structure that is duplicative: a movement in the second half of the book that echoes the first. John D. Haigh, in *The Fiction of C.S. Lewis*, his Ph. D. Dissertation at the University of Leeds (1962), suggests otherwise. He describes five parts: narrative framework (chs.1 and 2), Perelandran Eden (3-6), Temptation (7-11), Descent (12-14), and Ascent (15-17), divisions corresponding to the conventional literary divisions of exposition, development, climax, counterstroke, and eucatastrophe. Both paradigms are neat, and both make sense: in fact too much sense, more sense than matters either to Ransom or to me.

What would envelop me was an eloquence of writing and story-telling – I can only call it a rich economy – that I had never known before. Schwartz's strong book is on the philosophy behind *Perelandra*, deriving from Henri Bergson, little-remembered now (or so my colleagues in the philosophy department tell me) but quite the man in Lewis's younger days, a thinker to be reckoned with.

Bergson speaks of Emerging Evolution and the *elan vital*. On Perelandra that is spouted by the intruder Weston (the imperializing scientist from the first book) who will invite the fallen oyarsa of Thulcandra, the 'silent planet', to inhabit him, thus hoping to move ever upwards and outwards in the cosmos. (I had already read my Milton: here was a creature who was no longer pleased merely to "reign in Hell.")

56

My problem with the Schwartz analysis is not incredulity (there is a torrent of learning in the small book, especially in its footnotes) but irrelevance: I just do not care – and neither would Ransom, who in fact is repelled by the thought, or would Lewis, I think, for whom it is 'machinery'. What I would come to see – and this pretty quickly – was Ransom's *spiritual* growth, that is, a maturation of character and spirit, undulating certainly, like the waves of the Perelandran sea, but always slanting up. Thus only one mode or organization, I believe, matters: *Ransom's own spiritual development*, no matter the tergiversations of his challenge.

His ability to see, know, and understand, whether it be of physical danger, moral seriousness, and especially cosmic consequence, *and to act* (there again is the prescription of spiritual theology), grows and grows. That growth compels him beyond himself, heroically. And because he was skeptical of himself *but went on*, I believed in him. That is, he had my trust, my allegiance, and my assent to what he was learning and would do. That assent would reach other precincts of the Perelandran world.

I offer another favorite passage, from Chapter Two, that made me think, How long can C. S. Lewis continue to startle me? There Lewis provides a physical emblem of Ransom's development, as rudimentary sensations compel us (that is Ransom and me) to make sense of data until a conception of the whole is complete. Recounting what Ransom has told him, Lewis reports:

> He seems to have been awakened . . . by the sensation of falling. . . . The next thing he noticed was that he was very warm on one side and very cold on the other. . . . [B]oth were soon swallowed up in

the prodigious white light from below which began to penetrate . . . the walls of the casket. Lewis offers some inferences along the way: His first impression was of nothing more definite than of something slanted. . . . And even that lasted only an instant. The slant was replaced by a different slant; then two slants rushed together to make a peak, and the peak flattened suddenly into a horizontal line. . . . At the same moment he felt he was being lifted. Up and up he soared till it seemed as if he must reach the burning dome of gold that hung above him instead of a sky.

The sensations gather, we knowing no more than Ransom, until he, and we, know that he is swimming upon a sea.

Though a strong swimmer he is scared almost, but not quite, witless. Then something rushes past, narrowly missing him. When he is at the crest of a wave he sees it below, "an irregularly shaped object with many curves and re-entrants. It was variegated in colours like a patch-work quilt – flame-colour, ultramarine, crimson, orange, gamboge. . . . This thing might have been thirty acres or more in area." And here is an irony. I can still see that object, vividly, even though I am color-blind (and had never heard of 'gamboge'.)

Slowly, by a sort of perceptual logic, Ransom and I put together the visual, kinetic, auditory, and thermal sensations that added up to that heaving sea with floating islands upon it here and there. (C. S. Lewis would tell us that the entire story began with an image of those islands.) The author had plopped me down into a sensation-rich but conceptless environment and compelled me not only to survive but to make sense of it. My relief when Ransom finally made it onto one was palpable: a storm was gathering.

And there is the pattern of the entire book: Ransom (and

I) seeing more, knowing more, understanding more – at great risk – until we reach the summit of metaphysical knowledge afforded by the planet, by its tutelary spirit, the very Oyarsa Perelandra, and by the new king and queen of that world, Tor and Tinidril. In her "The Vision of Cosmic Order in the Oxford Mythmakers," Marjorie Evelyn Wright emphasizes hierarchy, courtesy, and obedience in the works of Charles Williams, J.R.R. Tolkien, and in the Space Trilogy. All three qualities apply, increasingly, to Ransom, bearing him further and further out. He is the providential man.

Not long before reading *Perelandra* I had rushed through Fitzgerald's translation of *The Odyssey*. For his physical prowess, resourceful cunning, rhetorical adroitness, sheer virility, desire for adventure, hunger for wonders and, yes, for his blood-thirsty vindictiveness (when his arrow goes through those rings I could see the bloodbath coming, and every one of those suitors would get his comeuppance), Odysseus became and remains my all-time second-favorite hero (ahead even of Tarzan, almost all of whose books I had read years before). Why my very favorite hero, and that by far, should become Ransom, an anti-Odysseus if ever there was one, is easy to explain.

His courage had to be dredged up, and it was a *moral* as well as a physical courage; he risked all and endured all on behalf of others, on behalf of a whole world in which he had no palpable stake, and he was unarmed, at least physically. Who would *not* want to be *him*? I certainly did not care to be tested as Ransom was, a test far graver than any faced by Odysseus. But I knew that although I lacked Odysseus's prowess, I was armed, however meagerly, as Ransom was, with will, brains, and a moral compass. (Although I have been tested, I also understood, even when young and semi-feckless, that *being* armed and *using* arms are two different states of being.) And yet, as heroes go, Ransom is more or less unheralded.

On my first visit to Wheaton College, wherein resided the "Lewis Collection" – invaluable, but nothing close to what the Wade Center would become – I met the greatly hospitable Professor Clyde Kilby, its founder, whose *The Christian World of C. S. Lewis* I had devoured. I told him of my work on *Perelandra* and of my upcoming visit to Oxford, where I hoped to interview Walter Hooper. He gave me both his own notes (!) on *Perelandra* and a letter of introduction to Walter: my scholarly life, with it networks, interviews, archival research, holograph letters, and collegiality (I was already a veteran of stack-prowling, with all its contentments) had begun.

In that light I've been reading about Lewis and his works continually. To my surprise I have not found much devoted solely to *Perelandra*: chapters, sections of chapters, a few articles. Chad Walsh, who wrote the first book on Lewis, claims, puzzlingly, that the theological debate is tedious but maintains the reader's interest; then, but oh-so-fleetingly, writes that Ransom, "recognizes that his own identity and destiny are at stake." And that's it.

In his elegantly written book John Lawlor, a Lewis student who knew him well, reminds us that the debate between Ransom and the Unman is intellectually, psychologically *and spiritually* dispositive, even though Ransom thinks it all "unfair . . . unfair." Lawlor brings great clarity by showing how Lewis draws upon Boethius's *Consolation of Philosophy* and his reconciliation of God's Foreknowledge with our Free

Will. Lawlor quotes: "The thing was going to be done. . . . The future act stood there. . . . It was a mere irrelevant detail that it happened to occupy the position we call future instead of that which we call past." And like Lawlor, William Luther White (*The Image of Man in C. S. Lewis*) understands that what is at stake is more than one man's identity. He reminds us that the Unman (once the great scientist Weston, we recall) would "spread spirituality," that is the "life force," to which Ransom answers that he knows little about "the religious view of life" since he happens to be a Christian!

I have saved Colin Manlove (*C. S. Lewis: His Literary Achievement*) and Thomas Howard (*C. S. Lewis: Man of Letters*) for last; they are to my thinking the most insightful critics of *Perelandra*: would that each had written a whole book on it. Manlove unpacks Ransom's broadening understanding with great economy by reminding us that the world is richer, especially in its denizens and their habitations, than Ransom thought. (I recall the entourage progressing just below the surface of the water in *The Voyage of the 'Dawn Trader'* but having nothing to do with the adventure.) "By gradual transitions we traverse the entire hierarchy of being from abstract shapes to the inanimate and thence to the animate, and so up to the human who is monarch of them all. It is like approaching a throne," and that, indeed, there is a third party to Ransom's conversation with the Green Lady, namely Maleldil, who is filling her mind with knowledge. About a third of the way into his book, Manlove strikes gold: "what is myth on our world becomes fact in Perelandra." Ransom is not having a mere adventure.

Howard reminds us that escape "from the silence of our

own world into the clarity and luminescence of another may be to find ourselves suddenly face to face with our own story." Of that clarity and luminescence on Perelandra Howard shows that landscape is no mere backdrop but "the fabric, or locale, necessary to the drama itself." Furthermore, he reminds us of Lewis's narrative device, that the story is being recounted after-the-fact. Thus "all that happens in Perelandra is told to the 'earthbound' Lewis – all "those glories and splendors that have so ravished him and that Lewis fears." Howard continues, "At least part of the drama, then, has entailed Ransom's progress from fear to desire in the presence of the bright realities, and Lewis's posture as a beginner here keeps this before us," his surrogates.

I remained pinned like a butterfly to a card. My belief, my consent, at least my literary consent, had a mooring. Certainly there are nits to pick, like the 'mal' (evil in many languages) of Maleldil. And why a *Green* Lady, a color denoting bad luck in medieval fantasy? I know: fertility. But that is too on-the-nose. No matter, I believed *in* her, not least for her innocence, credulity, and intelligence, and in Ransom, and in the world.

A few years before writing about *Perelandra* I had developed the healthy custom of reading more than one book (sometimes three or four) at the same time. At a point in the late Sixties these clustered around the layers and contours of 'belief', a compelling interest to a student of rhetoric and of literature (I had been an undergrad English Lit major, after switching, for entirely non-literary reason, from Spanish Lit). I believed in Heathcliff and Elizabeth Bennet and Don Quixote and even in Tarzan, but *Perelandra* invited, even seemed to compel, a different sort of belief, more akin to believing in Jesus, and yet *He* was nowhere to be seen.

My interest was directed to the Yale Studies on persuasion, tiresome social science but not unhelpful. More helpful, in fact dispositive, were I. A. Richards's *Practical Criticism*, along with Wayne C. Booth's landmark *The Rhetoric of Fiction* and Lewis's own *An Experiment in Criticism*. Richards taught us, among so many other items, to pay attention to the four vectors of meaning: sense (the plain subject), tone (attitude towards material), feeling (attitude towards reader) and intention (the author's objective). Since a pre-condition of belief is meaning – some connectedness – I could now examine Lewis's meaning. Here the plot thickened considerably.

First is Lewis's own tendency towards obliqueness; he ever wanting to steal past the "watchful dragons" of self-consciousness by "smuggling" theology in "under the guise of fiction." Of course, Christian beliefs are everywhere in *Perelandra* – incognito; just as Lewis thought God is everywhere though "everywhere incognito." Of course I saw that, especially after having read *Out of the Silent Planet*. But, my goodness, the layers of insulation! There is C. S. Lewis, then 'Lewis' the actual narrator of the story, then Ransom, who is recounting it all to Lewis. The effect of all this is that C. S. Lewis disappears. Just whose sense, tone, feeling and intention are in play?

Booth teaches us about narrators and narration, reliable and otherwise. C. S. Lewis has worked overtime – including real people – to anchor 'Lewis's' tale in the bedrock of actuality, all towards enhancing our trust in Ransom and the credibility of his incredible tale. Booth has also taught us to look to the 'implied author', the one every reader takes for granted, but *this* author is not implied at all but explicit: he is that 'Lewis', skeptical, weak of nerves but brave, *admiring of Ransom*, whom he trusts implicitly – *in spite of his incredulity*: one of us. (More than once does Lewis interrupt in his own voice to interpret or wonder over what Ransom has reported.)

What am I being asked to believe? The story and I occupy the same space-time continuum; and – remember, Ransom already has returned – it is being told in the here-and-now. The events, and more importantly, the *consequentiality* of the events, are actual. Might something be expected of me? Ransom had always thought that doing battle with Powers and Principalities was a sort of Bible-speak, but now . . . ?

What C. S. Lewis achieved was new to me. The loss of my mother at a young age – its effect on me, my father and my older brother – was tumultuous. The world shrank, my church-going became formulaic, my praying virtually ceased. For reasons that have no place in these reflections I was frightened, lonely and isolated, notwithstanding the presence of a father who was attentive, good-humored, resourceful, brave and, deep within, sad.

Two changes brought me out of the funk. Finding C. S. Lewis was the first; the second was meeting (on a blind date, no less) the woman I would marry. She became the companion I longed for. She and Lewis generally, but *Perelandra* especially, gave me hope – allowed me to Hope (reinforced exponentially by *The Chronicles of Narnia*). The world was no longer as small as I, and something vastly important was at stake in my reading, thinking, and imagination.

Meanwhile, the force of the narrative was overwhelming,

so the question of meaning would wait. Wayne Booth taught me that three basic interests compel a typical reader. (Lewis, though differently, says nearly the same.) The first is *cognitive*, the excitement of discovery. Who can resist asking, What happens next? In reading *Perelandra* one never knew, though no matter what it is, *it makes sense once you see it*, and you certainly do *see* it. The second is *qualitative*, an interest marked by a satisfaction that comes from completion (of, say, cause-effect or a fulfilled promise).

Lewis delays the effect, building the cause slowly and in stages and largely by way of Ransom's responses to the world and to event. The payoff – it's almost blasphemous to call it that, but as stories go, that's what a denouement is – goes far beyond any expectation the reader may have had. The third is *practical*, our interest in the characters, our judgment of them, perhaps our struggles beside them.

I did not struggle next to the Lady, at least not at first – the Green Lady, the color of the witch in *The Silver Chair*, the color, I'm told, one should never wear to a wedding. I wondered about her, pulled for her, was slightly vexed by her (by Maleldil? Can't He get *on* with it?), and I was unsettled by the Un-man's Argument from Vanity, exerting an allure that I found creepy, credible, and possibly disastrous.

Rather I struggled next to Ransom, for the simple reasons that 1/ his struggles were somehow my own, an extra-literary, perhaps a non-literary response, but mine nevertheless and one I think intended by C. S. Lewis; and 2/ though I already knew he'd made it back, I did not know the price he would pay or how he would pay it. The practical interest was very strong.

When Ransom debated the Un-man I mentally marshaled arguments on his behalf, and – I had done some boxing – when he hauled off and launched a straight left hand lead to the Un-man's chin I nearly whooped out loud. (So much for "words, words!") I had experienced the glorious visual splendor of the planet; the undulating excitement of its sea and the challenge of balance on a floating islands (I would have told Ransom to stay on the balls of his feet); the wonder of its creatures that should have been grotesque but (as Ransom saw) were not, nor even dangerous, but happy, even loving; its globular fruit and juice: who would not want more and more of *that*? (But Ransom intuited, and I believed, that such repetition would be an abuse.)

All of this, though, was in the past tense, filtered through the gauze of time: it was being recounted. What would follow, albeit narrated in the same mode, remains eerily present: in one instance, that of Ransom in the cave, time seems to stop as he battles real and imagined menaces; in the other, on the mountain, time disappears. Here in later chapters I explore those episodes; they are of a different key, or at least made me a different sort of reader. Then (and still) I affirm the world, its occupants, its threat, its hero, and his apocalyptic challenge. I believe in those.

'Lewis' says of Ransom that he is "sane, and wholesome, and honest." Ransom is *decent* – even at my first reading that word and its referent were going out of fashion, but it is meant to be recognizable. In rhetoric it is called ethical proof, meaning trust attending to the source of the message, in this case Ransom. And there is Ransom's own code: he must not take that second taste, or, more to the point, he cannot allow the miserable pleas of Weston – a moment when the Un-man allows him freedom within his own body – to go unheeded.

So I saw that this code, what I would learn is Natural Law, is built into Perelandra, too. I recognized its morality, a response to which, in the form of conscience, would be pivotal in Lewis's conversion. Isn't that why he begins *Mere Christianity* with examples of unfairness that all of us understand as *wrong*? This code is here, is in the whole universe, and Perelandra is no exception. This is not Tormance, David Lindsay's planet in *A Voyage to Arcturus*, where good and evil are fungible and which so impressed Lewis (and scares me, along with very many others).

A style marked by imagery incrementally accumulated, a reliable hero, tetherings to the world I know, a bedrock of morality, and a yarn that compelled immersion in its telling are all together enough to make any reader believe in the *gestalt*, but they are not all. Why would a thirteen-year-old girl write to Lewis asking for Ransom's address so she could thank him? The answer lay in Lewis. I had already carefully studied a very great, very neglected Lewis book that quickly became a primary tool of any literary criticism I would practice. I came to regard it as highly as a book which, ironically, Lewis disliked intensely, Aristotle's *Poetics*.

In *An Experiment in Criticism* Lewis teaches that a literary object is both something made (*poiema*) and something said (*logos*), the former conveying the latter. The "something said" can have a Realism of Presentation *and* a Realism of Content, as does, say, *Pride and Prejudice*. Or it might have a remarkably believable Realism of Presentation but not of Content, as is the case with *The Odyssey*. Or, as with *Perelandra*, it may have the first and make us overlook that we don't quite have the second, perhaps asking, "or do we?"

Lewis cites mistaking some imaginative construction for reality as the most extreme form of fantasy. Well, I was not doing that. But it did not matter. The unactuality of Ransom's Perelandra journey *is and remains irrelevant to my belief,* which lies elsewhere. At the other extreme is Morbid Castle-building by the unliterary: only the barest notional assent is ever given. The mid-ground, though, is Normal Castle-building. In that response the reader is either Egoistic, "always the hero and everything . . . seen through his eyes," or Disinterested: "the day-dreamer is not the hero of the day-dream or perhaps not present in it at all."

Spectating is quite different. Think of a boxing match, especially if you have boxed. You wince at this blow but bob beneath that one, all along shouting advice to your favorite. You manifestly do *not* want to be in the ring, and life goes on after the bout. Perhaps pity and fear, as Aristotle suggests, have been exorcised. But then the difference. The match has almost certainly showed you nothing important, certainly nothing permanent, whereas great fiction really does enlarge the spirit, often permanently.

It does so, I believe, by engaging three levels of belief. The first is *literary*: I believe this *as I read* it because it is vivid, plausible on its own terms, and it practices "the art of bringing something close to us, making it palpable . . . by sharply observed or sharply imagined detail," as Lewis tells us. The second level of belief is *imaginative*. We achieve some epiphany, a breakthrough into some other dimension of thought or sensibility, so that when the story ends, the insight, feeling, and perhaps some new belief – some change – lasts. It is real.

Wordworth's *Prelude* did this to Lewis, MacDonald's *Phantastes* did this (and much more) to Lewis and to me. The third level of belief is *spiritual*, conveyed by awe and marked, finally, by holiness: we are fully immersed in the numinous. Here *The Magician's Nephew* never fails me.

Still, we must remember the reader's role. A profitable one is

> not thinking about any such generality as human nature. Attention is fixed on something concrete and individual; on the more than ordinary terror, splendour, wonder, pity, or absurdity of a particular case. When such stories are well done we usually get . . . what would be probable if the intitial situation occurred.

Not long after that passage, Lewis describes stories "impregnated with life," with "the flavour or 'feel' that actual life has." There is Lewis's famous *Kappa* element. The good authors "allow us temporarily to share a sort of passionate sanity." And there am I.

So in addition to style and the like, how does Lewis do it? The answer (we are still in *An Experiment in Criticism*) is, this way. A literary object must represent

> the triumphant adjustment of two different kinds of order. On the one hand, the events (the mere plot) have their chronological and causal order. . . . On the other, all the scenes or other divisions of the work must be related to each other according to principles of design, like the masses in a picture or the passages in a symphony. Our feelings and imaginations must be led through 'taste after taste, upheld with kindliest change'. Contrasts (but with

premonitions and echoes) between the darker and
the lighter, the swifter and the slower, the simpler
and the more sophisticated, must have something
like a balance, but never a too perfect symmetry,
so that the shape of the whole work will be felt
as inevitable and satisfying. Yet this second order
must never confuse the first.

Upon first reading this passage, I felt meta-theoretical scales
drop from my eyes, saw planets line up, heard gears grip into
place. My understanding of art deepened exponentially, and
then so did my judgments and appreciation.

What I did not at first realize, or realize for quite a
while, is the application of that passage *to the whole of Lewis's
body of work*. I have read other authors devotedly, examined
them assiduously: Sigrid Undset, Robertson Davies, Austen
and the Brontë's, Mark Helprin, the inexhaustibly engaging
Thornton Wilder; I have lost myself in worlds: Chaucer's,
Shakespeare's, Dr. Johnson's. But none compelled me, not
only to re-visit but to write and speak about the author and
his work here, there, and everywhere I was invited, in a high
school classroom or on a nationally televised documentary, for
pay or for free as did Lewis.

Some people map out a career, a 'path', but I was too
far in even to know I was on a path. Other interests claimed
my attention – rhetoric, American public address, Peruvian
culture and its paradigms of communication, *conversation*
– and I've written on all of them. But none displayed the
amplitude of Lewis in his genres, modes of expression
(formal argument, casual suggestion, exposition, description,
narration, verse short forms and long . . .) all at a routinely
high level, nor displayed his range and depth of thinking, or,
simply, his brilliance. Why do I not tire of this man (who

proved nearly as interesting as his work)? I even tried putting him aside for a spell: no luck.

The more I read and re-read Lewis the more I realize that each of his works, and he himself, are "related to each other according to principles of design, like the masses in a picture or the passages in a symphony." My thoughts, with my "feelings and imagination [were] led through 'taste after taste, upheld with kindliest change'." Before I knew it I had produced a body of work relating to him. And then . . . and then I saw that the Whole Man was in one book.

What we must recall of Lewis is what Henry James said of Shakespeare: *nothing was lost on him*. (An idea might gestate for decades before he put his pen to it, at the same time he writes out other ideas in other books.) For example, his assimilation of Christian cosmology and its use in the trilogy was exhilarating: I already had taken enormous imaginative comfort in that model of the universe. "If the angels (who I believe to be real beings in the actual universe) have that relation to the pagan gods" – Why not? I thought – "which they are assumed to have in Perelandra, they might *really* manifest themselves in real form as they did to Ransom."

The Green Lady, though, posed quite a challenge. "She's got to be in some ways like a Pagan goddess," he wrote to Sister Penelope on November 9th, 1941, "and in other ways like the Blessed Virgin." I now recall the weeks I spent on the *Screwtape* manuscript and one of his very few corrections there. Uncle Screwtape tells his Nephew that each human male has two versions of a woman in mind, "a celestial and an infernal" one." Except he doesn't: 'celestial' became 'terrestrial', probably to avoid *any* implication of our Blessed

Mother. I saw that conceptually I had moved from cosmology to a classical-*cum*-biblical *Weltanschauung* seamlessly.

Meanwhile the sea undulated as Ransom and I continued to discover: the dramatic otherness of the new world was gripping. He met the Woman and learned of her world, her restrictions, her husband far removed, the Voice that taught her but refused to direct. Her choice would be her own. He began connecting the dots and so was unsettled, especially when he realized that *he was the miracle*. He debated then fought then pursued the horror of the Un-man, whose facile and arbitrary sadism he had witnessed – as I had. (In fact I remembered it from my boyhood, looking into eyes that "did not defy goodness but ignored it to the point of annihilation.")

These combinations of colors, contours, and experiences; of psychology, cosmology and angelology; of rumination, drama, and violence (both on a floating island and at sea); of Ransom finally killing the Un-man during a horrific ascent in darkness; his emergence into a world so fresh and beckoning, so utterly glorious – all swept me along through peaks and troughs and loops of excitement, elation, fear and satisfaction.

Words, images, and rhythms; discoveries, risks and a rooting interest apocalyptically consequential; characters in an Other, perfect world yet tethered to my own space-time – all this finally enraptured me, and continues do so. But the voyage began with . . . 'Lewis'. Remember.

On his way to meet Ransom, he "had to bite my lips to keep myself from screaming" in the fog and cold, this after thinking, "why should Ransom not be a dupe?" He, like Ransom later on Perelandra, gives himself many reasons not to go on. And yet, "somehow or other, despite the loathing and dismay that pulled me back and a sort of invisible wall of resistance that met me in the face . . . almost shrieking as a harmless spray of the hedge touched my face, I managed to get through the gate. And there I was . . . wringing the handle and shouting . . . as if my life depended on it."

His bravery, the sort C. S. Lewis would have witnessed in the trenches of the First World War, is stirring. Only after the fact does he learn that the attack was actual, from forces determined to keep him away. (To add to the verisimilitude, Lewis the scholar cannot resist, of all things, the insertion of a footnote, explaining "the celestial frame of special references" in his source.)

Lewis's harrowing journey pre-figures what is to come. Ransom, too, will wonder about his fitness, will feel alone, and will doubt, but he will also debate a being that needs no sleep, and then he will fight. He will learn that, though he "is the miracle," he is *not* alone, for a voice tells him, "it is not for nothing that you are named Ransom," and later, "My name also is Ransom." Not many of us have had such an epiphany, but many of us have had our rationalizations "snap like a violin string." He must fight, he will be mauled, he will probably lose. It doesn't matter, for no matter that "he might beg, weep, or rebel . . . sing like a martyr or blaspheme like a devil. . . . The thing was going to be done." Further, he will see that "what was before him appeared no longer a creature of corrupted will. It was corruption itself. . . . The joy came in finding at last what hatred was made for."

A decade later, while re-reading *Perelandra*, I was smacked by Lewis's use of 'joy' in that sentence. By then I had read *Surprised by Joy* and knew a deal about *Sehnsucht*.

I had read *Till We Have Faces* (Lewis's greatest purely literary achievement, or so he and I thought and think, or have I already said that?). At the top of a mountain (another mountaintop!) Orual hears a voice, "Why should your heart not dance?'" She goes on. "The sight of the huge world put ideas into me, as if I could wander away . . . wander forever. . . . the freshness and wetness all about me . . . made me feel that I had misjudged the world. . . . as if its heart also danced."

Of course we readers of the book know that, but then Lewis drops the hammer: "I ruled myself," writes Orual, straight into denial, just as she will later deny seeing the palace in the valley.

But for Ransom, as for me, there would be no denying. About two-thirds into the book, after Ransom knows, understands, and has accepted what he must do, the key, so to speak, changes (that is, one becomes more dominant than others), as though only now does the real adventure, the real test, begin, and it will not be merely a terrified walk through the woods to a cottage, as it was for 'Lewis'. Ransom, too, changes, into something of an epic hero.

More mentally and physically fit than he had been, maybe ever in his life, he is settled in his determination, utterly convinced in his righteousness. In one Tarzan book, the Ape-Man finds his house ruined by the Germans and, grimly, says, "now Tarzan make war." That is not Ransom. He will simply get on with it, like the Englishman, God bless him, that he is. (I know, Tarzan is Lord Greystoke, but *not* when in his Tarzan mode.)

C. S. Lewis will ascend with him. Leaving behind the Green Lady, like Dante's Matilde in *Purgatory*, he heads for

Paradise, however tortuously. That mystical vision will come, not easily in the book nor, probably, in his life. He has taken me from a ravishingly beautiful and dramatic landscape to the very face of evil itself, through wonders both strange (flora, fauna, the Lady) and familiar (the tergiversations of a humble but convicted mind) into darkness – one, by the way, he would himself know within a relatively few years, and one I've known.

In the letter to Mrs. Hook he writes this: *Perelandra* "works out a *supposition*. ('Suppose, even now, in some other planet there were a first couple undergoing the same that Adam and Eve underwent here, but successfully.')" Yes, as in the debate – another debate – in the Underworld of *The Silver Chair*. Suppose Narnia *is* an invention, argues Puddleglum, invented by children playing games, still that supposition beats hers, the witch's, real world hollow. Or as we pray in Hebrews 10:23, *"Yet keep us firm in the hope we profess because the one who made the promise is faithful."*

And just there is my belief. We have an "if-then," but if you *begin* with the "then" – what you long for, what you know is true – mustn't the "if," instead of preceding it, follow? That is, if there is the 'then' – the glories of Heaven – the 'if' cannot be far behind. And so because I believed that Heaven is real – there it was in the book and all along in my imagination and spirit – I believed in *Perelandra*, which somehow got me there. That new dominant key, not so by-the-way, would be Myth.

CHAPTER IV

Myth

belief 'that'

Belief that something is true seems at odds with that something at the same time being a 'myth', usually regarded as fiction. But what if the myth, as Lewis learned, is also fact? The myth would be a pattern into which the fact fit, or from which it emerged: "a description or story," Lewis wrote to his friend Owen Barfield, "introducing supernatural personages . . . not connected with any given place or time."

Its apprehension is subjective. His famous late-night talk with J.R.R. Tolkien and Hugo Dyson, however, showed him otherwise; *at the same time* a myth could be a fact in time, objective. He was on his way to becoming a Christian believer and would write the essay (later incorporated into *Miracles*), "Myth Became Fact."

I wondered, How does that work? In *Pilgrim's Regress*, John meets The Man, who provides an answer. "'Child, if you will, it is mythology. It is but truth, not fact: an image, not the very real. But then it is My mythology. The words of Wisdom are also myth and metaphor. . . . But this is My inventing, this is the veil under which I have chosen to appear even from the first until now. For this end I made your senses *and for this end your imagination* [my emphasis], that you might see My Face' – an image most important to Lewis, as we see in *Till*

We Have Faces and, tellingly, at the end of *Perelandra* – 'see My Face and live.'"

Myths, then, are depictions, analogies, 'supposals' (a favorite Lewis word). In "Shelley, Dryden, and Mr. Eliot" (1939) Lewis explored the concept: "[it] is thus like manna," he writes, "it is to each man a different dish and to each the dish he needs. It does not grow old nor stick at frontiers . . . and even from the same man at the same moment it can elicit different responses at different levels." That conversation with the "hardest boiled of all atheists" in 1926 epitomized this conception. "'All that [anthropological] stuff . . . about the Dying God. . . . It almost looks as if it had really happened once.'" That is, the shape of the story – a god coming down among us, dying, then rising again – had a resonant allure.

This, in my case, clicked the Gospels into a proper intellectual perspective. We have the Fact, the incarnation of the Great Myth, that is, His myth, in fact Him. So *Perelandra* is *not* an allegory; things are exactly what they seem to be, and the only correspondences are supposals. In fact, it occurs to me that the book is an allegory inside out. What is literal on Perelandra – the myth actually enacted there – would be seen as allegory on Thulcandra. Here we have it, as Ransom ponders the task before him:

> When the Bible used that very expression about fighting with principalities and powers and depraved hypersomatic beings at great heights. . . . it meant that quite ordinary people were to do the fighting . . . Your idea that ordinary people will never meet the Dark Eldila in any form except psychologically – as temptations or the like – is simply an idea . . . it may be anyone's job to meet them . . . in some quite different mode.

Ransom's battle – and the cosmic significance of it – is the real thing.

Lewis allowed that the imaginative man in him was older than the religious man. He would learn from his 'second friend' Owen Barfield (who learned nothing from Lewis) that the imagination is the organ of meaning, that is, the organ that connects us to truth. Thus the power of great myth: to fuel the imagination. Isn't that why Leonard Bacon, reviewing the book for *The Saturday Review of Literature*, could write:

> He has a powerful, discriminating and, in the proper sense of the word, poetic mind, great learning, startling wit, an overwhelming imagination . . . and the capacity to express himself best described by saying: 'he can write' . . . One's own fancy, one's own thought, leap after the writer's. Agreement, dissent, analogy wake in the lethargic mind. . . . Mr. Lewis' romance, or better myth, for Mr. Lewis' imagination (as has been said of a very great poet) is equal to the manufacture of myth, is . . . *provocative of the suspension of disbelief* [my emphasis]. . . He knows how to make the fantastic explicit.

But it isn't easy.

The most difficult kind of world to evoke is a mythic one, for such a world has its own rules, its own history, and its own ambience; its life is utterly foreign to the life we know on earth. It is most truly an Other world, which is why Lewis chose a literal *other world* to embody the Christian Myth, and which is why he wrote (in "On Stories"):

> No merely physical strangeness or merely spacial distance will realize that idea of otherness . . . you must go into another dimension. To construct plausible and moving "other worlds" we must draw on the only real "other world" we know, that of the

spirit.

– which describes my experience, as well as that of so many others.

Although *Perelandra* possesses all the narrative elements that could elicit belief, these elements are not responsible for the effects evoked by the story of Perelandra. Whether or not we see through Lewis's strange names to the more familiar figures they represent, or are able to recognize Biblical parallels or those to Milton's *Paradise Lost* or to Dante's *Commedia*, most readers of *Perelandra* share an other-worldly experience. Myth should be judged according to the criteria of Mythopoeia, for only myth "conveys the meaning embodied in itself." Although I do sympathize with Ransom – even, in a sense, identify with him – a projection of myself into the character is unnecessary for mythic purposes, for mythic characters, Lewis writes, "are like shapes moving in another world. We feel indeed that the pattern of their movements has a profound relevance to our own life, but we do not imaginatively transport ourselves into theirs."

Moreover, though the experience of myth may be sad or joyful it is always . . . something else, and certainly is for me, as Lewis continues in an *An Experiment in Criticism*:

> The experience is not only grave but awe-inspiring.
> . . . It is as if something of great moment had been
> communicated to us. The recurrent efforts of the
> mind to grasp – we mean, chiefly, to conceptualize
> – this something, are seen in the persistent
> tendency of humanity to provide myths with
> allegorical explanations. And after all allegories
> have been tried, the myth itself continues to feel
> more important than they.

So it is that *Perelandra* gives the impression of having hit rock bottom, of having exposed some Reality with which there can be no dispute.

No, the myth is not itself the Reality, but after experiencing it we are compelled to say, "these images have struck roots far below the surface of my mind" – they do, indeed, depict something which "*may have been* historical fact." Above all, a myth is extra-literary, which is why its simple narrative may be got at through any number of authors.

Even if we would not care to live in Perelandra (though I certainly would visit), it yet manages to arouse those "lineaments of ungratified desire." The generosity, charity, and innocence, the commerce with animals and with spirits, and the delicious and willing sensual pleasures – each stimulates in us a vague longing, a desire, our very own *sehnsuch*t, a feeling attendant upon a realization that no particular thing, no matter how much we thought we really wanted it, can ever genuinely gratify, because all longing is for the same thing: God and Heaven.

Put another way, it is "spilled religion," and the drops may be full of blessing to the unconverted man who licks them and begins searching for the cup whence they spilled. In short, the power of *Perelandra* derives from the fact that it offers a convincing portrayal of that Truth for which, knowingly or not, we have always longed.

This Reality and the longing it arouses exist permanently, independently, and unconditionally. That is why this utterly extra-literary phenomenon (what Lewis called the Dialectic of Desire), if "faithfully followed, would retrieve all mistakes, head you off from fake paths, and force you not to propound, but to live through, a sort of ontological proof." *Perelandra* is a part of such a proof.

I was no stranger to the phenomenon. At a very early age dinosaurs seemed mythological; a bit later astronomy took hold, cosmic dimension suggesting a very great truth beyond my ken. Soon I discovered Edith Hamilton's *Greek Myths*, then Roger Lancelyn Green's books. Somehow I knew that not all of these were in the same plane, the same order of reality, but dinosaurs and sidereal years seemed no less real than Zeus. In middle age I came upon quantum physics. Talk about a myth!

Well, we don't have to; just ask Einstein. The cosmos is ruled by gravity, but the particles that make it up have none. And then there is "spooky influence" at a distance – a very great distance. And so I've concluded that *we* are a Myth. How we must look to the angels! Do they tell each other stories about us, perhaps collected in anthologies?

Stories, always stories. The story of the dinosaurs, of the universe, of the atom, of the frog prince . . . All alike seemed to me to be Wonder Tales – and still do. The *Wonder Tale* includes such genres as the fairy tale, fantasy (fairy tales for adults, as Lewis described *That Hideous Strength*), some science fiction (so-called), old-school gothic tales (e.g., ghost stories), much children's literature, and even some horror tales. Of course, national mythologies are included, but non-miraculous legends (e.g., Robin Hood) are not. At the center lie obvious titles: *The Chronicles of Narnia*, most of Grimm, the Alice books, and Tolkien's *oeuvre*. Away, but not very far away, from the very center, is Chesterton's *The Man Who Was Thursday* (and maybe, just maybe, the novels of Charles

Williams).

I do not believe beast-fables per se belong within the circle, but exceptional ones (i.e., *The Book of the Dun Cow*) make it in. An interesting example is *The Wind in the Willows*; there is an element in Grahame's great work that gives pause (see the magnificent chapter "The Piper at the Gates of Dawn"). Thus it happens, I think, that the breadth of this meta-genre is such that, near its fringes, parts of books not otherwise wondrous pull the work into the Wonder ambit.

At the very fringe, farthest from the center, are such works as Acts and the Gospel of Mark, the realism of which serves to highlight the *outbreak* of wonder, as though wonder and its effective causes were lurking everywhere but ultimately derive from a central source, Our Lord.

Of the features typical of wonder tales these are, I think, closest to the center of the concept:

1/ right and wrong (and often Good and Evil) are concrete (though perhaps not explicit): events show the world to be neither a pinball machine, nor even a plant, even less a tick of Tourrette's, but the issuance of a Moral Intelligence;

2/ spatial (and less often temporal) dimensions are small: e.g. a kingdom might be walkable in two or three days;

3/ marvels (esp. visual ones) abound, although these may not seem wondrous within the tale;

4/ forests, often perilous and magical, appear frequently;

5/ prohibitions, usually one very pronounced, are prominent;

6/ traditional tales can withstand even bad tellings, and commonly are embodied in a signature telling;

7/ very often the wonder world is marked by order and hierarchy: i.e. they are medieval;

8/ the familiar is comfortably rendered, expectations (in this respect) being satisfied;

9/ natural axioms are altered (e.g. animals talk), though not randomly;

10/ the morphology (this from Tolkien) is usually tripartite: escape, recovery, consolation;

11/ the protagonists (and perhaps others) often undergo some transformation of social station, marriage, or family;

12/ signs, often subtle, are central;

13/ desire, *Sehnsucht*, is common;

14/ a character's identity, either stolen, mistaken or forgotten, is often at issue;

15/ a sense of "remote proximity" is common: long ago perhaps, but not necessarily far away, and certainly not inaccessible; and

16/ they may prepare us imaginatively for the Gospels, the greatest of Wonder Tales. Numbers twelve through sixteen especially mark the boundaries of my sub-genre. Myth, the wonder tale, and *Perelandra* overlap considerably.

I saw that fusion in the work of two men whose collective influence had run high indeed, that of the anthropologist Sir James George Frazer and of the psychologist C.G. Jung. Represented syllogistically, the argument would be:

Major Premise

Psycho-racial archetypes, described by Jung as permanent residents of the human spirit, are rhetorically effective when posited in a work.

Minor Premise

The critical symbols of Perelandra closely correspond to psycho-racial archetypes, observed by Frazer to be historical phenomena.

Conclusion

The critical symbols of Perelandra effect a strong and affirmative response, i.e. are persuasive.

We know that Lewis knew both. Frazer's *The Golden Bough* demonstrates the commonality of religious practice and belief among cultures varying widely in time and place, while Jung's work identifies the archetypes that mark the species. The similarities between many of those – practices and archetypes – and events occurring in *Perelandra* are striking, often identical.

For example, the idea of an incarnate God – Maleldil himself when he came to Earth – was common to the Washington Islands, Egypt, India, Polynesia, and Greece (exactly as the atheist Weldon had realized). That a woman could provoke vegetation and that *sacred nuptials* could lend even more bounty to the land was a belief widely held. Thus the wedding of the Green Lady to the King will permit those parents to "be fruitful and multiply" in ways so magnificent as to be nearly incomprehensible to us:

> We will fill this world with our children. We will know this world to the centre. We will make the nobler of the beasts so wise that they will become *hnau* and speak . . . When the time is ripe for it .

. . we will tear the sky curtain and Deep Heaven
shall become familiar to the eyes of our sons. . .
. I set forth even now on ten thousand years of
preparation – I, the first of my race, my race the
first of races, to begin. I tell you that when the last
of my children has ripened and ripeness has spread
. . . it will be whispered that the morning is at hand.

A major conceit of *Perelandra* is the occupation of
Weston's body by the Devil. Frazer tells us that an old and
widespread belief (including Christian) holds that a body may
be victimized by an alien spirit after its own soul has departed.
During Ransom's journey upward through the mountain,
Weston's body is finally destroyed when it is thrown into a
raging blaze (fire imagery being important throughout this
scene); Frazier tells us that Fire Festivals were common in
Europe, their purpose being either destruction of evil spirits
or purification. Only after this ascent through darkness and
fire is Ransom prepared – we might say 'purified' – for the
glory which follows.

The Golden Bough impressed itself on Lewis at an early
stage, but I do not suggest that he had the book open at his
elbow, nor that it is a 'key' to *Perelandra*. (Any of Lewis's
books have too many keys to count.) Moreover, would he
have needed it at his elbow to weave his mythic tapestry?
What he absorbed, he used. And we need not know, nor even
know of, Frazer for those elements to resonate with the reader
– and that for a most particular reason.

We have no direct evidence that Lewis read the
Jungean sources of my discussion: *The Spirit in Man, Art, and
Literature, Psychological Reflections, Mysterium Coniunctionus,*
or *Psychology and Religion.* But he very probably knew *The
Archetypes and the Collective Unconscious,* at least by way of

Maud Bodkin's *Archetypal Patterns in Poetry: Psychological Studies of Imagination*, which he was reading in 1940. Jung is descriptive, his ideas working through literature whether we know it or not, because they, like the images documented by Frazer, *are at work in us.*

Thus the combination of Frazer and Jung seems to be a sort of template. For example, since art derives from psychic motives, Jung tells us, "we would expect a strangeness of form and content, thoughts that can be apprehended only intuitively . . . and images that . . . are the best possible expressions for something unknown – bridges thrown out towards an unseen shore." Had he read *Perelandra*? These "expressions" (primarily representations of the psyche) become Myth when taken together.

The constituents are those archetypes, primordial images that constantly occur in the course of history and appear wherever *creative fantasy* (Jung's term) is freely expressed. The moment of their appearance is always characterized by a peculiar emotional intensity, "as though chords in us were struck that had never resounded before, or as though forces whose existence we never expected were unloosed."

At such moments "we are no longer individuals but the race . . . Whoever speaks in primordial images . . . evokes in us all those beneficent forces that ever and anon have enabled humanity to find refuge and to outlive the longest night."

The twentieth-century view of the universe should be especially hospitable to archetypes, Jung wrote, for although "heaven has become an empty space to us, a fair memory of things that once were," our heart nevertheless "glows, and secret unrest gnaws at the roots of our being." (Note: that

Sehnsucht-sounding description is, again, Jung, not Lewis.) We should (practically and morally) accept archetypal symbols, not as arbitrary signs standing for known and conceivable facts, but as "an . . . expression for something supra-human and only party conceivable." Though few such symbols may appear in a particular work, if they are well-chosen their cumulative effect could be irresistible.

Moreover one of the most impelling archetypes is the life of Christ, which, claims Jung, describes in symbolic images the events in the conscious (and transcendent) life of a man who has transformed his higher destiny. As the reader shares in this victory, he reacts strongly against the Satanic (fourth) element of Jung's Trinity-archetype. That the drama of Christ is clearly the center of all of us is a *psychological* fact, he says. And immediately below this numinous level lives the King, the carrier of Myth who represents a superior personality, a "statement of the collective unconscious." The King "represents the daylight of the psyche" – *all this, again, is Jung, not Lewis.*

Apparently, says Jung, mankind has no choice concerning archetypes. "'Principalities and powers' are always with us; we have no need to create them even if we could. It is merely for us to *choose* . . . We do not *create* 'God' we *choose* . . .him." Or as Ransom himself hears it – this bears repeating:

> You are feeling the absurdity of it. Dr. Elwin Ransom setting out single-handed to combat powers and principalities . . . But when you come to think of it, is it odder than what all of us have to do every day? When the Bible used that very expression about fighting with principalities and powers . . . at great heights . . . it meant that quite

the ordinary people were to do the fighting.

Quite explicitly, then, we have no escape, for, according to Jung, the "ideas of moral law and of the Godhead are parts of the indestructible constituents of the human soul."

That is why only myth "conveys the meaning embodied in itself" (again, Jung). Furthermore, although we do sympathize with Ransom a projection of ourselves into the character is unnecessary for mythic purposes. "We feel that the pattern of their movements has a profound relevance to our own life."

Whether or not we 'see through' Lewis's method, most readers of *Perelandra* share a numinous experience, because there, with our inverted allegory, where abstractions are vibrantly alive and not emblematic, myth and actuality are one, exactly as Lewis had intuited by way of his famous late-night talk with his friends.

In *The Discarded Image* Lewis describes the medieval cosmic model. I had already met it and had come to love it; I find it beguiling. Who would not delight in the image of concentric crystalline spheres, each inhabited by a tutelary spirit – spirits corresponding to pagan gods, or to angels? I know, of course, that planetary orbits are not circular but elliptical, and that the earth is not at the center of the system. But I also know, from Lewis, that the earth's medieval location made it the deadest, not the most important, of the heavenly bodies. And I know that *they* knew the earth was round and that very great distances separate heavenly bodies.

That is, pre-Modern man got many *facts* wrong but got much right. For example, they believed in *longeavi*, preter-naural beings of many varieties – as on Perelandra. Remember the scary creature in the cave, going about its business and having nothing to do with Ransom's adventure? – rather like our octopus, fantastic by any measure.

The model is adapted into *Perelandra*, *mutatis mutandi*, and I believe that it is true. Because myths, like the Christian myth, can be true. There really is a hierarchy of angels. Some of them are among us. A fallen angel has brought great evil into the world and so corrupted it. Yes, things may have gone otherwise, but, in the event, we have indeed been ransomed, bought back by the intervention and sacrifice of God Himself. The medieval model is not science, but I believe that, in some form – a form we will experience at the end of the book and of the world – it is real. That is, Lewis's adaptation of the medieval model, so perfectly fitted with the Christian model and its angelology, renders me credulous.

Certainly I was pre-disposed to belief, but now the symbols and substitutions; the correspondences (both within my psyche and within the cosmos); the struggles, risks and engagements (including with powers and principalities); the past and the promises of what is to be – all *cohere*. Lewis made my hope concrete, and that is why I believe that the spiritual model is real.

As with his probabilistic style, Lewis's psychological movement proceeds inexorably, "from the curious to the frightening to the beautiful the ravaging and terrifying and finally to the utterly serene and ecstatic," all in spite of thinking we want glory but knowing it is the very thing we cannot tolerate, as Tom Howard so aptly sums up an ascent of knowledge and achievement. Not long into his adventure, Ransom gets it. He has burst a "shimmering globe," been bathed in an ice-cold shower, and his nostrils have filled

> with a sharp shrill exquisite scent. . . . A re-
> enchantment fell upon him. . . . If a naked man
> and a wise dragon were indeed the sole inhabitants
> of this floating paradise, then this also was fitting,
> for at that moment he had a sensation not of
> following an adventure but of enacting a myth. To
> be the figure that he was in this unearthly pattern
> appeared sufficient.

And I, necessarily, am next to Ransom, having gone out of this world to the inside of another, with a pattern of delight, menace, risk, and consequentiality – rather like a meta-story from which other, more local, stories emerge.

At a relatively early age Lewis concluded that the heart of Dante's *Commedia* comes near the end of the *Purgatorio*, where there is an unfallen earthly Paradise. There Dante meets Matilda, a resident of that garden. We read (ll. 37-42, Esolen translation):

> My feet stopped, but my eyes went wandering over
>> The far side of the river, marveling
>> At all the fresh and various blooms of May,
> When there appeared, as now and then something
>> Will suddenly appear and lead astray
>> Anything else you might be thinking of,
> A lady all alone who went her way,
>>> Singing and culling flowers in the grove,
>>> Or at her feet the dappled blossoms lay.

And just there begins the heart of Ransom's adventure.

Before his first conversation with the Green Lady Ransom has a dream: "the dream (for so it seemed to him) of having lived and walked on the oceans of the Morning Star rushed through his memory with a sense of lost sweetness that was well-nigh unbearable." How fleeting is Joy! But not on Perelandra; rather it is living as a state of innocence and must allow free will. The Green Lady will make her own choice: not divinely uninformed but not divinely assisted, either. Ransom's only task in that choosing is simple: remove impediments to her existential freedom. Like Lewis, she will have her own version of a bus riding along the High.

For a long spell I lived with my family in a New York suburb: superb schools, K-12. My children were taught by gifted people; my son in particular had an English AP teacher who was unmatched. She and I became friends, and eventually Ellen thought to invite me to speak to her classes when she had assigned C. S. Lewis (and some others). So several times I discussed *Till We Have Faces* and *Perelandra*. Of course the students were top shelf, and by the time I visited she had laid a considerable foundation. Now, Ellen and I went to the same church, so we both knew that, to some degree, she was " stealing past those watchful dragons."

Sometimes the students' questions – concerns, really – were daunting. Considering his power, isn't Maleldil too passive? (Well, he respects the Lady's free will, and he did get Ransom – the miracle – to Perelandra.)   Why is the ending so monotonous? (Perhaps because you're too young?) How is the underground 'beetle' Ransom's equal? (They are both creatures, created beings, legitimate occupants of their respective realms.) Who is Lewis's 'voluble self'? (That would be Ransom's talkative – read Lewis's – talkative nature, which, as we have seen, often had to be quieted.) Why is the Lady

92

and not the King tempted? (We do not know that he wasn't; moreover, he is being prepared and therefore, presumably, protected.) If Perelandra is the pinnacle of perfection why is there an underground, apparently evil, cave? (Why not? The 'beetle' creature might wonder why there is any world *other* than a dark cave, with all that nasty light!) What gives Ransom the right to kill the Un-man? (The same code that *obliges* him to do so: the Un-man is a parasite preying upon innocence, and, lest we forget, Weston is virtually dead already.) Why can't dragons speak? (Yet? Of course, it does communicate.)

These few questions fairly represent the very many questions I heard from students over the course of several visits. I haven't omitted any that had to do with any feelings of mystery (as opposed to suspense) or of the numinous. My reason is sadly simple: there were none. Near the conclusion of a visit, I would invite remarks on their emotional, perhaps even spiritual, responses.

Only very seldom did anyone care to admit to any feeling approximating Joy. Maybe, as Lewis has said, such a response is so private as to be embarrassing if reported aloud. I know I have kept mine to myself, unless I've been among a small group of people who know what I'm talking about. Then again, my own response has blossomed over decades. *Perelandra* is a mature book that, as Lewis has instructed, must be read in the 'same spirit as the author writ', that is, by mature readers. So, No, I answered a last question, Lewis did not intend it for children.

But for the childlike? I've come to believe that the students were over-thinking, as advanced high school students are wont to do. What they did not see, or look for or respond to, is this, from *An Experiment in Criticism* (its Chapter Five being my source on myth for much of this chapter):

> Even at a first hearing it is felt to be inevitable. And the first hearing is chiefly valuable in introducing us to a permanent object of contemplation – more like a thing than a narration – which works upon us by its peculiar flavor or quality, rather as a smell or a chord does.

By way of a network of metaphors Lewis manages to embody universal principles and properties, thus uniting whole classes of concepts: theological, cosmological, psychological. Early in the fourth century Martianus Capella wrote a curious work, *De Nuptius Philologiae et Mercurii*, On the Marriage of Learning and Eloquence. *Perelandra* is an offspring of that marriage. As with most children so with myth: we may detect the father's eyes or the mother's coloring, but the child is essentially itself. It is combinative. The hyper-analytical students, it seems to me, generally missed that synthesis.

A useful question is, Where? Yes, we know: the planet Venus. But that is a literary answer. The actual place is the reader's imagination and, thereafter, the spirit. I recall Lewis teaching us that imagination is the organ of meaning, which I take to . . . *mean* . . . an identification of the dots and their connections, through the gateway that is the imagination, into the spirit. That, for example, is what happens to Orual in *Till We Have Faces*. That novel is no myth, nor even a "myth re-told," as Lewis himself claimed, but a modern novel – until its last section. There Orual, her defenses worn thin, enters that inner precinct of meaning, and there she lives her myth, which is also fact.

I felt that same sort of appeal when I first read *The Great Divorce*. A bus trip to Heaven? My cuppa! Yet even in that short, explicitly didactic fiction Lewis evokes a world of wonder: grass that doesn't bend to the slight foot of a mere wraith, for example. His passengers are brought *into* that world, the front porch of Heaven. Unlike Ransom, they are *not* the miracle; the bus ride and its destination are. *It* cannot fall, but their Fall can go on, unless . . . And there am I, different characters at different stages of my own life, Lewis's x-ray machine finding me out, his imagination showing me what is at stake.

For me, *The Great Divorce* came a year before *Perelandra*, *Till We Have Faces* some five years after. They (and much else in Lewis) *fit*. But only *Perelandra* not only invites but compels my hope, my belief.

> Or were the old myths truer than the modern myths? Had there in truth been a time when satyrs danced in the Italian woods? . . . It was strange to be filled with home-sickness for places where his sojourn had been so brief and which were, by any objective standard, so alien to all our race. Or were they? The cord of longing which drew him to the invisible isle seemed to him at that moment to have been fastened long ago, long before his coming to Perelandra, long before the earliest times that memory could recover in his childhood, before birth, before the birth of man himself, before the origins of time.

Later, under circumstances crushing in their glory, the King says, "Nay, in the very matter of our world, the traces of the celestial commonwealth are not quite lost. Memory passes through the womb and hovers in the air. The Muse is a real thing." I believe we call her The Holy Spirit.

That epiphany, however, comes with a price, for Ransom, for Lewis, and perhaps for the reader. We are fallen; spiritual formation requires strife.

CHAPTER V

Strife
depletion and resolve

Lewis had told us that the real challenge of creating a new world is that, eventually, *something has to happen.* So about a third of the way into Ransom's adventure, during a conversation with the green Lady, something does happen. Ransom blurts out, not in the Old solar language but in English, "'By Jove! What was that?' She also exclaims. "Something like a shooting star seemed to have streaked across the sky . . . and some seconds later an indeterminate noise reached their ears."

I am as startled as they are. Something had "'fallen out of Deep Heaven'," as the Lady said, and shortly thereafter "a single wave passed under their island," a foreshadowing of the strife to come. In the moment, though, they – Ransom because of the Lady's calm response: "her face showed wonder and curiosity" but, so rarely on our planet, no fear – they are calm. Perhaps the King would know what has happened, and to find him they must go to another island, a great distance away. No bother, says the Lady, we will simply each ride a fish, which the Lady beckons. They cannot then know – though we, the readers, have some inkling – that just here Ransom's great struggle has begun.

Lewis's psychological insights are everywhere, and everywhere organic, though casually posited. During a spell in their conversation, the Lady, startled, asks Ransom, "but how many of you are there?" – after learning that almost all Thulcandrian land is fixed! This sort of casual emotional realism, surprising in its novel point-of-view, marks the book throughout, as it does most of Lewis's narratives. It does not surprise or even intrude. What does surprise, however, is an audacious stroke a few pages after the big (if still distant in mind and space) event, and it is something I had not noticed until my second reading.

The denouement of *Perelandra* occurs at the peak of the mountain on the fixed land; there Ransom is afforded the awful privilege of witnessing the Great Dance (mountains and dance being recurring images in Lewis's work: there is my next, and last, chapter). Earlier, though, not long after the distant event that will change everything, the Lady brings Ransom to the fixed land. He witnesses all sorts of creaturely wonders as they climb.

And so, at this second reading, I thought, Did Lewis shoot his bolt here? Why give the reader *any* taste of the wonder that is to come some one hundred and fifty pages later?

> The circle of the golden sea below them was now spread out in an enormous expanse and the green rock pillars above seemed almost to overhang. . . . Down below, on the islands, though one had not remarked it at the time, there must have been a continual background of water noises, bubble noises, and the movement of beasts.

After much climbing – hard, that is for Ransom, not for the gymnast that the Lady seems to be – his perspective is entirely altered, an effect that Lewis employs frequently: the world is not as it first seemed.

> A high, singing wind carried . . . a cooled and refined quintessence of all the scents from the richer world below . . . [making] one continually conscious of great height [just *how* high Ransom would learn, paying dearly for the ecstatic privilege] . . . . He took a few paces forward into the cathedral spaciousness of the plateau. . . . 'Let us examine the sea,' she said presently. . . . The richness of its colours – its orange, its silver and purple, and (to his surprise) its glossy blacks [the same black we've seen on certain creatures on Malacandra?] – made it seem almost heraldic.

And just here I am reminded of that moment, in *Till We have Faces*, when Orual, high on a Glomean peak, has her soul swept away by the beauty of the world and thinks how wrong she may have been her whole life. In fact, it is Joy itself that fills her: a glorious epiphany – until we read perhaps the bleakest words Lewis ever wrote. "I ruled myself," right into denial.

On Perelandra, too, the moment is ruined for Ransom and the Lady. "About two miles off, dark against the coppery-green of the water, there was some small round object. . . . It appeared to be perfectly spherical; and he thought he had seen something like it before." Lewis, in description and conversation, will slowly draw out the approaching menace that is Weston, who had dispatched him to Mars and who now seeks to imperialize the cosmos on behalf of what he thinks is the Life Force. He simply does not, cannot, comprehend what lies behind *that*.

The strife that follows builds slowly, and within that gloaming unto night does Ransom come to grasp the actual purpose of his journey. Abstractly, it is this. In her rewarding *Lost in Thought: The Hidden Pleasures of an Intellectual Life* (Princeton, 2020), Zena Hitz writes, "asceticism – sacrifice and suffering for the sake of some good – is fundamental to our dignity. . . . To be driven by a desire to . . . wonder . . . takes determination and work, *or the good fortune of an externally imposed deprivation*" [my emphasis]. There is the beginning of spiritual theology, which Lewis practiced his entire adult life.

If your mother dies when you are eight years old (or nearly ten, as in Lewis's case), and you watch your older brother go to pieces and your father suffer miserably (but bravely and internally), you don't quite see Hitz's point. But you will. The fuses differ in length, and the bombs that explode concussively differ from each other, but the suffering and struggle – whether or not you recognize its source – are palpable. The clinical and theoretical literature on early parental loss is sizable, and if (as I did when preparing *Branches to Heaven*) one reads through it, you see that Lewis and, I found, I and my brother were very near stereotypical case studies.

For Lewis that was the beginning. He was a snob, a liar, almost certainly an adulterer, and a bigot. We often forget what he converted *from*: he had a tortuous road to become what Walter Hooper called, "the most thoroughly converted man I've ever met." After that conversion he had his alcoholic brother and the steadily declining and increasingly obnoxious Mrs. Moore to contend with, as well as a vocation he simply could *not* lay down. Certainly he had his delights, but professionally he suffered and his health was compromised.

Moreover, and not so by-the-way, he suffered the enduring horrors of the Great War trenches as well as embedded, painful shrapnel. To this I add a comment made to me by the delightful and generous but puzzling William Nicholson, whom I interviewed during a lunch break at the set of *Shadowlands*, which he wrote. Why, I asked, did you choose to write on Lewis? His answer stunned me and stuns me still: "because Lewis reminds me of me. Like him I did not know commitment or suffering until middle age." I thanked him for his time.

Withal somehow you find, as did Lewis and as does Ransom and as I (and my brother, near the end) did, that you are not alone and that by the alchemy of Grace and the support of a cloud of witnesses not only shall all be well, but you will have done much good that otherwise might have been left undone.

All of the Christian devotional writers agree, and Lewis had read and re-read many of them, from St. Augustine and Walter Hilton; to Thomas a Kempis, St. Francis de Sales and William Law; and his own contemporary Evelyn Underhill. (And we must not forget Chesterton and MacDonald.) All his life CSL lived along that road: devotional writers of fiction and non-fiction.

As much as any other lesson, *Perelandra* renders this one: "Those sufferings bring patience, patience brings perseverance, and perseverance brings hope, and this hope is not deceptive because the love of God has been poured into our hearts by the Holy Spirit which has been given us." (Rom 5:5)

Devotional witnessing, instruction and inspiration come in many forms: imaginative, expository, analytical, argumentative, sermonic. In that light, just as Lewis could be enlarged by his sources, I look back on him as mine.

Almost every book, every essay, as well as many of the poems, catalyzed an epiphany, kaleidoscopically, whether intellectually, imaginatively, emotionally or spiritually.

He teaches me, for example, of the solidity of Heaven (in our present state we are too insubstantial even to bend a blade of its grass); the eternal splendor (or horror) of every human being because none of us is 'ordinary'; the multiple-tasking of language and ritual (ours being too poor to embody the richness of supernatural glories); the inner working of myth, that "could have been historical fact" (if only Ham had let the unicorn into the Ark!); how we do not really want a father in Heaven but a grandfather, who will simply spoil us (personal note: I would have said grandmother, thinking of my own and of my wife); how the self is a prison we must escape, even when enjoying imaginative literature (oh, to know the olfactory world of a dog, he tell as us at the end of *An Experiment if Criticism*); how we not only *want* it "both ways" but *have* it both ways, that is, both a God in Heaven *and* Incarnated here with us; how our perspective must be transcended, historically, culturally and personally, as in *The Screwtape Letters* and elsewhere); how imagination is the organ of meaning, so that its synthesizing function reveals how this world prepares us for the next (as does Narnia).

But on Perelandra conversation and debate offer a different epiphany, not least in its resolution. The conversation between Ransom and Weston – the scientist is still himself – strikes me as banal, though Emergent Evolution and its Life Force were taken quite seriously in the first half of the twentieth century. In Lewis's hands it becomes a ruse: the fallen eldila of Thulcandra will use it to appeal to the pride, personal and professional, of the great scientist. He now speaks fluent Old Solar, explaining "'guidance, you know, guidance'. . . . He was squatting at the roots of his tree with his knees drawn up, and his face, now the colour of putty, wore a fixed . . . twisted grin. . . . 'Things come into my head. . . . being made a fit receptacle for it.'"

The thought of any devil has already been dismissed by Weston: "no real dualism in the universe is admissible." Ransom, remember, having said that he doesn't know much about what people call "the religious view" of life because, "'you see, I'm a Christian'," forces the issue until Weston proclaims that, yes, he would do anything the Force instructed him to do.

> Do you see, you timid scruple-mongering fool?
> I *am* the Universe. I, Weston, am your God and
> your Devil. I call that Force into me completely.
> . . .' A spasm like that preceding a deadly vomit
> twisted Weston's face. . . . As it passed, for one
> second something like the old Weston reappeared
> . . . howling 'Ransom, Ransom! For Christ's sake
> don't let them' . . . and he fell at Ransom's feet,
> slavering and chattering and tearing up the moss
> by handfuls.

Fleeing, Ransom thought "'if I lived on Perelandra . . . Maleldil wouldn't need to forbid this island. I wish I'd never set eyes on it.'"

He swims through darkness, not without some delight, until he comes to an island where he sleeps, only to wake in darkness to the sound of two voices. "'I am wondering,' said the woman's voice, 'whether all the people of your world have the habit of talking about the same thing more than once. I have said already that we are forbidden to dwell on the

Fixed Land. Why do you not either talk of something else or stop talking?'" And so the temptation to disobedience has begun, in speech. (I would learn the humor here much later: Lewis's friends knew him to belabor a point unto its last atom of meaning.)

Disobedience, argues Weston, now known as the Un-man, is what Maleldil wants, to know that you, he tells the Lady, are capable of the independence he has planned for you as the mother of a new race. What has disobedience brought you? Ransom asks the Un-man, who answers that it brought to Thulcandra the greatest gift, meaning the Incarnation. We have heard it all before: what greater good might have been granted had not The Fall occurred? We do not know, which is why we obey (a lesson I needed to learn). The Lady loses interest; Ransom realizes that, unlike himself, his adversary need not sleep.

This time when he wakes, he wanders and realizes that he is following a trail of mutilated frog-like creatures: ripped open but not dead – in an unfallen world death comes with great difficulty. When Ransom comes out of a wood he sees the Un-man tearing a creature down its middle, and their eyes meet.

> The face which he raised from torturing the frog had that terrible power which the face of a corpse sometimes has of simply rebuffing every conceivable attitude one can adopt toward it. . . . It looked at Ransom in silence and at last began to smile. We have often spoken . . . of a devilish smile. . . . not bitter, nor raging, nor, in an ordinary sense, sinister: it was not even mocking.

There I stopped. I would learn that Lewis had peered into the face of madness, that of Mrs. Moore's brother. But had he looked into a face smiling as the Un-man smiled?

I wondered, because I had, and Lewis gets it just right.

> It seemed to summon Ransom, with horrible naiveté of welcome, into the world of its own pleasures, as if all men were at one with those pleasures. . . . It was not furtive, nor ashamed, it had nothing of the conspirator in it. It did not defy goodness, it ignored it to the point of annihilation.

I've concluded since that much that we take for madness is actually demonic. Lewis continues:

> The children, the poets, and the philosophers were right. As there is one Face above all worlds merely to see which is irrevocable joy, so at the bottom of all worlds that face is waiting whose sight alone is the misery from which none who beholds it can recover

– leading "sooner or later either to the Beatific or the Miserific Vision." Ransom would conclude that this evil, on the outside, would challenge the rule of Heaven itself, but that at its core there is "nothing but a black puerility, an aimless empty spitefulness content to sate itself with the tiniest cruelties, as love does not disdain the smallest kindness." (A second, quite different face, will appear much later.)

The debate continued, with the Un-man playing the vanity card. He convinces the Lady to garb herself in colorful foliage and, in the water, to behold her own beauty. That, he argues, is the royal figure whom Maledil really expects to reign, once she has achieved what these days is called 'agency': "The expression on her face was noble" and "it was on those lines that the enemy now worked almost exclusively."

The protracted debate is psychologically complex, but Ransom could see the grand strategy. "The external and, as it were, dramatic conception of the self was the enemy's true aim. He was making her mind a theatre in which that phantom self should hold the stage. He has already written the play."

He knew – Lewis knew – that the most powerful form of persuasion is self-persuasion, because the Self is all-aggrandizing. Any salesman, preacher, advertiser, teacher, politician – any rhetorician at all – should read this section and tremble: this, Lewis seems to be saying, is what you are up to, this 'trumpery'.

What to do? Ironically, when alone Ransom tries some of it on himself, as is our wont. Losing the debate, and so the Lady, he reasoned that all he had to do was his best; "God would see to the final issue. . . . As for the fate of Venus, that could not really rest upon his shoulders. It was in God's hands. One must be content to leave it there. One must have faith. . . . " And then the hammer drops: "it snapped like a violin string." That is, spiritual theology teaches not only suffering and ascent but, between the two, *action*. Something must happen, and we (I, you) must do it. "Here in Perelandra the temptation would be stopped by Ransom, or it would not be stopped at all."

Alone, he wonders, How? and realizes that Weston's *body* can be destroyed. Though not a fighter he reasons that, physically, he was at no disadvantage, except for the long, sharp nails that the Un-man could wield. It would be a horror, certainly, but then Ransom hears a Voice, not unlike the one that spoke to John the Pilgrim in *Pilgrim's Regress*. "It is not for nothing that you are named Ransom. . . . My name also is Ransom."

At first the philologist in Ransom thinks this a coincidence, but by now he knows better. With "perfect certitude" he knows that by that time the next day he will have done the impossible. "You might say that . . . the power of choice had simply been laid aside" – like Lewis riding on that High Street bus or in Warnie's sidecar – "predestination and freedom were apparently identical."

The Voice tells him to sleep and that his sister sleeps as well and that he (the Voice) has cast the adversary into a sleep of his own till morning. The next day "some memory of boxing at his preparatory school must have awaked, for he found he had delivered a straight left with all his might on the Un-man's jaw."

I wonder how many readers have punched another hard in the face, either in the ring or out of it. I've done both and, I confess, it is thrilling to land a punch – fist tight, thrown from a shoulder turning in while rotating at the waist – just right, and to see its effect. Only one instance of it do I regret, but that is more than made up for by one of the faces being – years after the fact – the evil one that had beckoned me.

In Ransom's case the fight continues, Ransom motivated by "the energy of hating," in this instance lawful. "He felt that he could so fight, so hate with perfect hatred, for a whole year," even though he would soon discover that his back was in shreds. No matter. It was the Un-man who fled, to the sea and onto a fish. Ransom did the same in pursuit. Here I omit much of Ransom's thinking and sensation, except that he felt to be one with the marvelously muscled fish, "swimming in a bath of phosphorescence. He slept. Then he saw other creatures, following as in a celebratory parade. Yet "mere bigness and loneliness overbore him."

Then . . . then he had company. His own fish was swimming feebly, another slowly approaching. The Un-man sat upon it "hugging itself." It begged Ransom to speak to him, tears rolling down its cheeks. It asked what had happened, called itself Weston, and asked for help. Ransom asked if he were really Weston, the answer being "who else would I be," on the verge of tears. They converse, and Weston allows that a child frightened by a corpse knows more about the universe than all science and religion.

Yet, as the conversation goes on, he shows himself to be the same old Weston, reality is "neither rational nor consistent nor anything else." Soon Weston, hearing breakers ahead, panics. Ransom tells him to pull himself together: "say a child's prayer if you can't say a man's." Weston clutched Ransom's "hand . . . in darkness" and "had suddenly gripped his arm with both hands."

And so Weston, now the re-emergent Un-man, pulls Ransom down. "The water closed over his head: and still his enemy pulled him down into the warm depth, and down farther yet to where it was no longer warm."

Since my retirement I've been struck by the strangeness of a life unplanned. I was headed to law school, but after two weeks of college teaching knew where I wanted to stay. As a teenager I didn't date and was more or less intimidated by girls, whom I treated with almost comic (I was told) courtesy, and yet I married a sophisticated beauty at age twenty-one. When my dear son was himself twenty-one and, to my wife, seemed to lack direction, I spoke with him at her urging. "Son," I said, "when I was your age I married the woman who is still my wife and took the job that I hold to this day." He nodded, put his hand on my shoulder, and said, "gee, pop, I'm so, so sorry." Straight face. He thought I was telling a cautionary tale!

Here and there were Un-men and their snares. (For the record, I believe that demonic agents are actual.) But all along there was Lewis as a companion: the New York Society, my first lecture gig ($10 and supper), other speaking engagements, *C. S. Lewis at the Breakfast Table*, articles, TV documentaries, two other books, more speaking engagements, the Oxford Press Very Short Introduction – and always the Society: editing, chairing, lending a voice and an ear, moderating. None of it anticipated or designed. The same is true of my academic career. I was, with all the difficulties personal and professional, being watched over, first by Alexandra, then by a cloud of witnesses.

I noticed that one effect of early parental loss is detachment; one tends to spectate, as though an outsider (and often to self-destructiveness). I had some Dark Nights, certainly. Who has not? Is that not one of Lewis's many points? That Ransom and Orual, too, are us? But I never had a Dark Night of the Soul, or at least none that I felt as such. Lewis, however, did. Elsewhere I've noted the despair he describes to his pen pal, Fr. (now Saint) Giovanni Calabria. He is empty and, because tempted by pride, *hopes to stay that way*. But when Mrs. Moore dies he feels release, and not only imaginatively: he feels his sins are actually forgiven. Soon *The Chronicles of Narnia* pour into the world.

What matters here, I think, is the nature of a Dark Night. It is not marked only by despair; rather – according to St. John of the Cross, who lived it and wrote on it – it is marked, first, by purgation. That is followed, still in darkness, by ascent, as the soul moves through the Purgative to the Illuminative Way (the goal being the Unitive Way: a three-stage process common in the writings of mystics). In the first chapter of the second book of John's *Dark Night of the Soul* we read:

> . . . as [the spirit] goes forth from the aridities and trials of the first purgation . . . it is wont to pass a long time, even years. . . . in this latter state . . . . like to one that has come forth from a rigorous imprisonment; it goes about the things of God with much greater freedom and satisfaction of the soul, and with more abundant and inward delight than it did at the beginning. [But] it is never without certain occasional necessities, aridities, darknesses and perils which are sometimes much more intense than those of the past, for they are as . . . heralds of the coming night of the spirit. . . . after this manner . . . God brings the soul that He may lead it to Divine union.

Other writers – among them William Law, Walter Hilton, Dame Julian of Norwich, monumentally Richard Hooker, and, respecting the care of the soul, especially St. Francis de Sales – seem to be handbooks for Lewis: their advice, admonitions, prescriptions, and descriptions are everywhere in Lewis, and he makes no secret of his influences and sources. Orual – who, I think, does not make it quite as far (though she will, she will) as does Ransom – is virtually the personification of the three-stage mystical way. As readers, though, we are taken along with Ransom through a very dark night, fittingly subterranean in fact, the way many influences worked upon Lewis and work on us.

Ransom rises to the surface entangled with the Un-man, whom he finally kills. Believing the darkness is night he waits, only to discover that he is in a vast cave, that light will not come, and that now he must climb, blindly, from cliff to shelf, stumbling and stubbing, with only touch to guide him. When he did find a grip he "realised that he was now about to attempt some real climbing," not unlike "the most reluctant convert" in England, as Lewis described himself upon coming to the Faith.

Surely Lewis found guidance in Hilton's *Scale of Perfection*: "But this reforming is on two manners: one is in Faith only, another is in Faith and Feeling." The first wins one salvation, the second gets one to Heaven. "The first may be had, and yet the man may have together with it the stirrings and feelings of the image of sin." Indeed, the climb will bring uncertainties, including menaces both false and genuine. But "if he does not voluntarily assent thereto, he may be and remain reformed in Faith to the likeness of God."

Lewis's perfect metaphor – an exhausted climb within the darkness of a cave, an ascent marked by physical, psychological and spiritual struggle – may or may not (as we read) lead to that Faith and Feeling that "putteth out the liking in, and delight felt for sensual motions and worldly desires." The "old feelings of this image of sin" will be destroyed "and bringeth into the soul new gracious feelings, through the workings of the Holy Ghost" and finally "the bliss of Heaven."

First, though, the climb. Ransom does not fear starvation but thirst. He cannot help squinting to see further,

111

even though that act is futile and gives him headaches and creates "phantom lights and colours." When he makes it to a "wide horizontal surface" he walks so long that he fears he's been going in circles. "The starvation for light became very painful." Later "he heard a sound of water," a small waterfall with a stream. He refreshes himself and continues his climb. "Some real hope . . . began to enter his mind." And yet certain noises are troubling, "a dull plump" and a "rattling sound as if metal were being dragged over the stones." The Un-man? Or inhabitants of the cave, harmless but hardly agreeable? He decides to rest, and sees a "quivering luminosity" towards which the stream is leading.

After seeing that the light is a reflection from above he climbs to find it, thinking it probably a fire. The climb is tight and treacherous, but the cavern into which he finally enters is large. From a wide pit there rises a blazing fire, too bright and hot to behold. When he sits to collect his thoughts, he realizes that "they were collected in an unlooked-for way."

> Suddenly . . . like an attack by tanks, that whole view of the universe which Weston . . . had so lately preached to him took all but complete possession of his mind. He seemed to see that he had been living all his life in a world of illusion. . . . The beauty of Perelandra, the innocence of the Lady, the sufferings of saints and the kindly affections of men, were all only an appearance and outward show. What he had called the worlds were but the skins of the worlds: a quarter of a mile beneath the surface, and from thence through thousands of miles of dark and silence and infernal fire, to the very heart of each, Reality lived – the meaningless, the un-made, the omnipotent idiocy. . . .

Thus Ransom knew that whatever followed would come out

of that same hole he had climbed through, and he is right.

"'I thought as much'," he mutters. "It was the Un-man, of course: dragging its broken leg and with its lower jaw sagging open like that of a corpse." It raises itself to a standing position, but that is not all: "something else came out of the hole." Here Lewis provides the same sort of incremental discoveries that he used to paint Ransom's arrival on Perelandra, this time part by horrifyingly grotesque part: "a huge, many legged quivering deformity, standing just behind the Un-man so that the terrible shadows of both danced in enormous and united menace on the wall of rock behind them." Lewis had dreamt of bugs, which frightened him because their machinery seemed to be on the outside.

At that point a small grace drizzles in, as it will when we are in doubt. Ransom believes there is an attempt to frighten him, that the Un-man has beckoned the creature "and also that the evil thoughts which had preceded the appearance of the enemy had been poured into his own mind by the enemy's will." This insight awakens rage in Ransom. He approaches the Un-man and shouts, "'Do you think I'm going to stand this?'" He picks up a big stone and, ignoring a plea in Weston's voice, is "already upon it." And just then we hear the first real prayer of the story; "'In the name of the Father and of the Son and of the Holy Ghost, here goes – I mean Amen'."

The Un-man falls "as a pencil falls, the face smashed out of all recognition, and Ransom shoves the body over the edge into the fire below. In beholding the huge bug he finds his horror gone, asking "why one should quarrel with an animal for having more legs or eyes than oneself. All that he had felt from childhood about insects and reptiles died in that moment. Apparently it had all, even from the beginning, been a dark enchantment of the enemy's" – just like the assault on poor 'Lewis' at the very beginning of the book as he struggled to reach Ransom's house. Correlatives to one's life are prolific.

Now utterly exhausted Ransom resolves to sleep, there and then, not to go a step further, "'not to save my life. That's flat. Glory be to God, I'm tired.' A second later he was asleep."

On my second trip to Oxford my father came along. He had served at a military hospital during part of his service in World War Two and thought to visit his old barracks. He, Walter Hooper and I traveled by car, I driving and scaring them both. "St. Christopher jumped out a mile ago, Son!" Walter would laugh over that for nearly fifty years. My father would see his old barracks, but before that we stopped at the Kilns, Lewis's old home. There was Mrs. Miller, the Lewis's old housekeeper, doing as good an imitation of Uriah Heep as I would ever see even in the halls of academe. When we left, father allowed that he hoped neither of us would trust that woman. Walter simply grinned. Things are rarely as they seem, but sometimes they are obviously not.

Then again, sometimes they are. Ransom awakens slowly, decides to go on, though he knows not whereto, notes that he is in a great cavern, and, in the distance, sees more of the great beetles drawing a cart mounted by a form "huge and tall and slender," passing with "insufferable majesty." He thought, "assuredly the inside of this world was not for man. But it was for something." Another order of reality, again like the folk beneath the surface in *The Voyage of the 'Dawn Treader'*.

He experiences more strangeness, of a column of light

and of swiftly flowing water in which he, caught up, thinks he will die. Lewis's description of the visual wonders is striking, but Ransom is too hungry, weary, and resigned to death to note them well, so his report to Lewis (which of course we are reading) is sketchy. But "a moment later he was rushed out into broad daylight and air and warmth, and rolled head over heels, and deposited, dazzled and breathless, in the shallows of a great pool."

A great temptation here is simply to quote Lewis at length, such is the color, calm, and piecemeal recovery of Ransom. "There was mist and freshness and dew all about him," "streamers of bright vegetation." Eating passed into sleeping, then waking, then eating again and sleeping some more. He seems to have been "breast-fed by the planet Venus herself: unweaned until he moved from that place.

He could recall three impressions "of this long Sabbath": the "endless sound of rejoicing water," the "delicious life that he sucked from the cluster which almost seemed to bow themselves into his upstretched hands," and song, which "floated through his sleep and was the first sound at every waking," passionate, like a cello, but not "the passions of men." How long he remained in this lair is unknowable.

Feeling the need for some activity he carves on the rock surface, in Old Solar but with Roman letters, an epitaph for Weston, telling his story elegantly and fully and ending with the words, "The one thousandth nine hundredth and forty-second revolution after the birth of Maleldil Blessed Be He." As he journeys on, the planet becomes more and more gloriously comforting. "When he sat down he found himself in a new world."

We know Lewis was not a movie fan (though he did like *King Kong*). In that light I marvel at his cinematic effects. Movies are a visual medium, of course, and I know of only one writer as visual as Lewis, and he is Dante. But not simply that. The visual is intimately linked, as in the *Paradiso*, to the psychological and the spiritual discoveries of the observer; so much so that he becomes a participant in the scene – and so, then, does the reader. Our constant fugitive – Ransom, Lewis, maybe, someday, I – has traveled far in order no longer to flee. The price has been depletion, of his personal physical and mental resources, of time and space, even of any need to believe. But when he rises, refreshed in body and spirit, his faith is renewed. And he has brought us along into a precinct of supra-literary belief, of a 'belief that' where we will discover the absoluteness of holiness, more real than anything else that could possibly be mistaken for it, and available to us.

David Downing has convinced me that St. Paul is our first Christian mystic, though St. Stephen, as he is stoned and sees Jesus standing at the right hand of God, may hold that honor. Paul, who has ascended into the Third Heaven, talks about the experience reluctantly, which certainly sounds familiar. Still, Downing writes, "Paul did not consider his revelations a kind of spiritual accessory but rather the very foundation of his ministry . . . received by revelation from Jesus Christ."

Citing Bernard McGinn, Downing offers what the former considers "one of the most important passages in the history of Christian mysticism," 2 Corinthians 3:18: "And we, who with unveiled faces all reflect the Lord's glory, are being transformed into his likeness with ever-increasing glory, which comes from the Lord, who is the spirit." Downning quotes Underhill: "He who has seen the Perfect wants to be perfect too." There lies awe.

CHAPTER VI

Awe
beyond belief

In a letter, Lewis has cited the final cantos of Dante's *Purgatorio* as the center of the *Commedia*. He might have meant the vision of the Griffin-drawn chariot or of ladies approaching in dance in Canto Twenty-nine. Or he might have meant the very end: "From its most holy waters I returned/ as remade as a new young plant appears/ renewed in every newly springing frond,/ Pure, and in trim for mounting to the stars." (Esolen trans.) Will Ransom be *there*?

A mystic from early childhood, when he first beheld his brother's toy garden that provoked Joy, so Lewis remained, though (we recall) reluctantly. His imagination – his visionary prowess – pierced him to the core, right into his spirit. His apostolic calling compelled him to spread the message. His rhetorical prowess showed the world the result. He *seems* not to have had visions, as did Dame Julian, St. Teresa, St. Joan of Arc, or even William Blake. Perhaps the severity of his ratiocination – all the theorizing with Owen Barfield about the imagination and the intellect – aborted those. So his will – whether from modesty, or fear of uncertainty, or deference to those whom he regarded as his masters, or an apprehension of what might come next (the great mystics do not turn back) – his will held him in check.

In his *C. S. Lewis: Memories and Reflections*, John Lawlor has reproduced pages from Lewis's own copy of Julian of Norwich's *Revelations of Divine Love*, the point being to show the reader a sampling of Lewis's annotations. When Dame Julian writes, "speak of such men and women as for God's love hate sin and dispose themselves to do God's will," Lewis comments, "this whole book deals with those who have reached a really high degree of sanctity. *It would be rash to apply most of it directly to one's own problems*" (my emphasis).

Thus was his approach ever oblique. Dante, in the *Paradiso*, as throughout his work, names himself, but Lewis in his does not: he has dispatched Ransom, as though he were saying, "I'm just the messenger." But, then, how to explain this glory, from *The Voyage of the 'Dawn Treader'*?

> But now they could look at the rising sun. . . . What they saw – eastward, beyond the sun – was a range of mountains. It was so high that either they never saw the top of it or they forgot it. . . . And suddenly there came a breeze from the east, tossing the top of the wave into foamy shapes and ruffling the smooth water all round them. . . . what it brought them in that second none of those three children will ever forget. It brought both a smell and a sound, a musical sound. . . . they were seeing beyond the End of the Word into Aslan's country.

Or this, Ransom's long passage, from the nourishing pool where he recovers to where "the sea grew ever larger and the mountains less"? It is a place where "he dared not go" yet "dared not do otherwise." He thinks "this is the holiest place and the most unholy things I have ever done."

His perspective is utterly altered – classic Lewis – so that "the concave of the sea seemed to close him on every side" and the "rose-red peaks" are no longer distant. "Yielding without resistance to the awe which was gaining upon him, he walked forward with slow paces and bowed head." And there he discovers what he discerns will be the craft for his return to Earth. Ransom and we are gripped by that combination of what Otto named the *mysterium tremendum*, the *mysterium fascinosum* and the numinous: respectively, the fathomless mystery attaching to the sacred being, the deep enchantment of the worshipper as he contemplates that being, and his accompanying awe and fear before the sacred.

Now we are very close to the final, third, stage of mystical ascent. Following the strife of the purgative stage, along with its requisite action, and the illuminative stage, the unitive stage follows. In fact, we are about to enter that very region of awe, "in deepest solitude . . . a road right out of the self, a commerce with . . . the naked other, imageless (though our imagination salutes it with a thousand images), unknown, undefined, desired." In his *Poesias* the mystic St. John of the Cross writes:

> I entered in, I know not where, /And I remained, though knowing nought,/ Transcending knowledge with my thought . . . Of peace and piety interwound / This perfect science had been wrought /Within the solitude profound /A straight and narrow path it taught . . . / If you would ask, what is its essence – / This summit of all sense and knowing: / It comes from the Divinest Presence – / The sudden sense of Him outflowing . . . " (trans. Roy Campbell)

The writer of Hebrews (6:19-20) tells us "I will shower blessings upon you . . . we now have found safety . . . encouragement to take a firm grip on the hope that is held out to us. Here we have an anchor for our soul as sure as it is firm and reaching right through beyond the veil where Jesus entered before us and on our behalf."

That is how Ransom is blessed. Lewis, though, had to learn from George MacDonald's *Phantastes*, as he tells us in *Surprised by Joy*: "I did not yet know . . . the name of the bright shadow. . . . I do now. It was Holiness. . . . It was as though the voice which had called to me from the world's end were now speaking at my side. It was with me in the room. . . . I saw the common things drawn into the bright shadow."

Too long it was before I realized, at least consciously, that *this could mean me*. Soon after my first reading of *Perelandra* I came upon the following. In May of 1959 "Christian Spaceman – C. S. Lewis," by the influential critic and book reviewer Edmund Fuller, appeared in *Horizon*, an event, for its length and analytical richness but also for its prophetic insights. For example, in introducing Americans to the Space Trilogy Fuller makes the following tangential observation, so utterly surprising to us more than fifty years later:

> I rate high among Lewis's accomplishments a work *generally less well known* [my emphasis; this is 1959 remember], as yet, than the trilogy but for which I predict a growing reputation and a long life. This is the series of seven books for children which compose *The Chronicles of Narnia*.

He then gives a wonderfully inviting interpretation of *The Chronicles*. But he ends his essay with this appreciation of the Space Trilogy: "I am grateful to Lewis for some of my richest experiences of mind and heart," leaving us with choice imagery from Deep Heaven (*not* Narnia) and writing, "am I to say these are not real? I count [those books] among the great symbolic visions of ultimate reality which reveal to us that we are more . . . than the data our senses can record." Are *we* to say these are not Real?

How delighted I was to see Fuller cut through so much imagination-numbing analysis; namely, my own. "Lewis has used *epos*, the imitation of direct address, so the process may be described as follows." I then quote Lewis from *Miracles*: "On the other hand there is nothing against taking as your subject from the outset the adventures of a man who inherits an unexpected fortune. The unusual event is perfectly permissible if it is what you are really writing about."

I go on to say that the reader who is submissive to the conventions of 'speculative fiction', as well as being directly addressed as though in a report, "forgets his initial act of good-will ["a willing suspension of disbelief"] as such and accepts the doctrine embedded in the narrative: *those* beliefs are the norm." I still find this legitimate and useful, the way a brief plaque mounted on the wall next to *The Nightwatch* in the Rijksmuseum is useful, after a short while becoming useless.

My own first encounter with another world happened when (as I've mentioned early on) I was about three years old, and, in my case, my senses did record the event, for the simple reason that I embellished what I had seen. As I lay abed in my dark room I thought I saw the ceiling become gauzelike and that, just beyond that gauze, was a different . . . place. I named it The Potsiecombe, though I have no idea why. (Remote proximity: "just beyond" but also beyond all clouds, so the rain falls up.) I further discerned that it was populated, mostly by its king, a huge pandalike being named (though *not* by me, but by whom, then?) Moonie-ma-Moonlight, mostly, I think, because the moon was his favorite toy. I readily entered into the Potsiecombe and have since written its story (included in *Carry Me Home, Ten Tales for the Childlike*).

I never believed *that* an actual Potsiecombe exists, but I did, and do, believe *in* it – that *it* being the rampant presence, comfort, safety and joy ensured by a benevolent King who understands me implicitly. There was nothing numinous about the Postsiecombe, as there is, for example, in Grahame's landmark chapter "The Piper at the Gates of Dawn" in *The Wind in the Willows*. That is, it was surprising but did not seem uncanny to me. I might call it a half-way house.

Here is what I mean. Lacking any divine or god-like resonance, as the word 'numen' suggests in its use by Rudolph Otto, the Potsiecombe was a place of wonder, and one in which I could partake, but by no means did it fill me with awe; it was not, nor even close to being, holy, "the feeling," as Otto puts it (in *The Idea of the Holy*), that

> may at times come sweeping like a gentle tide pervading the mind with a tranquil mood of deepest worship. It may pass over into a more set and lasting attitude of the soul continuing, as it were, thrillingly vibrant and resonant. . . . It may be developed into something beautiful and pure and glorious. It may become the hushed, trembling, and speechless humility of the creature in the presence of – whom or what? In the presence of that which is a *Mystery* inexpressible and above all creatures.

It occurs to me that this resembles Longinus's 'sublime', in that (as he writes in Book VII of his *On the Sublime*) "our soul is uplifted . . . ; it takes a proud flight, and is filled with joy and vaunting, as though it had itself produced what it has heard." He continues, "for that is really great which bears a repeated examination, and . . . the memory of which is strong and difficult to efface. . . ." He concludes the section, "for when men of different pursuits hold identical views on one and the same subject . . . a concert of discordant elements makes our faith in the object of admiration strong and unassailable." And yet we know Longinus had not read Lewis.

Near the end of his adventure, the scale of Ransom's education rises exponentially, for he hears, somehow, the two eldila, Malacandra (an Oyarsa only on Malacandra) and Perelandra herself, the Oyarsa of Venus. Their appearances must be adjusted, of course, a frightening process, until they present as Masculine and Feminine, huge figures who seem to be racing to keep up with the spinning planet. "Pure, spiritual, intellectual love shot from their faces like barbed lightning."

He wonders about their appearance and is told that all his life he has known *only* appearances. He asks after the pagan representations of them how humans came to know of them:

> there is an environment of minds as well as of space. The universe is one – a spider's web within each mind [that] lives along every line, a vast whispering gallery. . . . Nay, in the very matter of our world, the traces of the celestial commonwealth are not quite lost. Memory passes through the womb and hovers in the air. This Muse is a real thing.

Could Jung's Collective Unconscious be real thing after all?

To do justice to the mythopoeic depth of the encounter I would have to quote it all. Instead I report a response: a vast, rich, fathomless realm has opened, not merely in my imagination but in my intellect as well. "This," I think, "*is* the realm of angels and of divinity, where my prayers go and are woven into the fabric of Reality, and are heard." In his *The Spiritual Life*, Adolphe Tanquerey writes, "many are His visits to the man of interior life," and I feel visited, with "a share in the divine life given us by the Holy Ghost who dwells in us, because of the merits of Jesus Christ."

Then Ransom sees approaching "a whole zoo of beasts and birds . . . pouring into a flowery valley" and senses that "the sense of ceremony deepened. The expectation became intense." There comes such a dawn that "each lily had its light and its dark side," for the shadows are piercing and cover the landscape. Then, "as the light reached its perfection and settled itself. . . . Paradise itself in two Persons, Paradise walking hand in hand . . . came in sight . . . and they walked down and stood on the far side of the water. And the gods kneeled and bowed their huge bodies before the small forms of that young King and Queen."

Thereupon Lewis raises the bar, almost impossibly, so much so that when reading this particular passage I feel as I sometimes do in the presence of the Blessed Sacrament. Here is a second Face:

> It was hard even for Ransom to tell me of the King's face. But we dare not withhold the truth. It was the face which no man can say he does not know. You might ask how it was possible to look upon it and not to commit idolatry. . . . so that almost you could wonder at finding no sorrows in his brow and no wounds in his hands and feet. . . . Here, where His live image, like Him within and without, made by His own bare hands out of the depth of divine artistry, His masterpiece of self-portraiture coming forth from His workshop to delight all worlds,

walked and spoke before Ransom's eyes.

I would find myself re-reading this passage many times, pondering it, and thinking, "what has Lewis seen?" For it (not alone but especially, not least in its audacity) convinces me that Lewis was raised to a visionary level of mysticism. Underhill calls such a vision "strange and terrible," for "few can bear to contemplate themselves face-to- face" with the Almighty. And yet, she says (and Lewis will agree) it is "rich simplicity."

St. Bonaventure rhapsodized about the face of Our Lord, for example in *The Journey of the Mind to God*, particularly chapter VII, and in *The Triple Way, or Love Enkindled*:

> His face worthy of the elders' reverence and the angels' desire. His face which fill the heavens with joy. . . . Yet His countenance remained quiet and humble. . . .

A provocative comparison to Lewis's overall description of Tor is with his own of Adam in *A Preface to 'Paradise Lost'*: "Adam was the first man in knowledge as well as in stature. . . . He was endowed, says Athanasius, with 'a vision of God so far-reaching that he could contemplate the eternity of the Divine essence and the cosmic operations of His Word'."

Tor tells Ransom how Maleldil taught him of the properties of bodies, and of good and evil; and he bestows names: "Tai Harendrimar, The Hill of Life," and so it shall be. Thereafter Tor talks of the future, for example freedom from Deep Heaven itself. "'And that,' said Ransom, 'will be the end?'" Tor's answer is beyond comprehension, to me at least: "'About that time we shall not be far from the beginning of all things.'" Then, after ten thousand years and their bodies having been changed, but not all changed, "'we shall be as the eldila.'" Tor calls what will happen neither an end nor a beginning, but the wiping out of a false start. Tor says, "'I tell you that when the last of my children has ripened and ripeness has spread from them to all the Low Worlds, it will be whispered that morning is at hand.'"

So far we have had an angel with a sword, wheels of fire, and other images from both the *Purgatorio* and Ezekiel. Tor's own descriptions have shown us much: for the literary believer, a vision of the medieval world picture; for the 'believer that', a report. Now, though, the mysticism becomes palpable: somehow Lewis must have *seen* what follows, and it is, as Downing so aptly puts it, "festive. . . . Lewis's vision is very much in this spirit, a kind of solemn and sacred revelry." It surely is that, a literary depiction of Lewis's delight in the medieval view of the cosmos, with the symbol of the *primum mobile* being "a young girl dancing with a tambourine."

Ransom is confused – who would not be? Is not the Incarnation "the central happening of all that happens? . . . Or do you make your world the centre?" The answer comes from eldilic voices, but he could not say who was speaking at any given time. "The dance which we dance is at the centre and for the dance all things were made. Blessed be He!" The voices debunk the grandeur of distance. "He dwells (all of Him dwells) within the seed of the smallest flower. . . . Deep Heaven is inside Him who is inside the seed and does not distend Him. Blessed be He!"

Nearly fifty years ago in *CSL: The Bulletin of the New York C. S. Lewis Society* (March 1975) Jaime Vidal reported a foundational influence in his "The Ubiquitous Center in Bonaventure and Lewis." Mr. Vidal, admitting that Lewisian references to Bonaventure are scant, leaves no doubt that the Canticle of the Great Dance echoes Bonaventure, but it echoes other as well. Alanus de Insulis (12th century) tells us, "God is an intelligible sphere, whose center is everywhere." Giordano Bruno (16th century) declared, "We can state with certainty that the universe is all center, or that the center of the universe is everywhere." Rabelais included the idea in his *Gargantua and Pantagruel*, and, earlier, it is there even in the *Romance of the Rose.*

Bonaventure provided a *schema* with our three-part way – Purgative, Illuminative, and Unitive – of mystical ascent. Elwin Ransom certainly moves through the first two, probably not the third (that is for Tor and Tinidril). But did Lewis? (Underhill, by the way, posits five stages.) Downing's summary of Otto's markers of the Absolute are Fear and holy dread; fascination and yearning; 'majestas'; intense dynamism; stupefaction; and mystery (absolute inapproachability).

These are all in Lewis's work (and earned him inclusion in Auden's anthology *The Protestant Mystics*). His vision is, as I've suggested, *sacramental, the pinnacle of Lewis's fugitive project, a work beyond a mere literary object. Here Lewis's literary artistry, reading, conviction, and worship are alchemized by his spiritual, that is his <u>mystical,</u> imagination. We are transported, like Ransom, to the very rim of the eschaton.*

Four revelations follow upon the knowledge that "He is not distended." "In the fallen world He prepared for Himself a body and was united with the Dust and made it glorious forever. . . . where this was enacted is the centre of worlds.

Blessed be He!" But soon, with our spiritual horizon driven farther than ever, we learn "The Dust itself which is scattered so rare in Heaven, whereof all worlds . . . are made, is at the centre. . . . Blessed be He!" Ransom hears that "an eldil is not more needful to Him than a grain of the Dust. . . . Love me, my brothers, for I am infinitely superfluous. . . . Blessed be He!" And finally this: "There seems to be no plan because it is all plan: there seems to be no centre because it is all centre. Blessed be He!'

Soon Ransom sees . . . something. In his recollection he allows that 'seeing' is inadequate. Each figure became the master-figure, serpents of light appear, and "minute corpuscles of momentary brightness" – "secular generalities of "peoples, institutions, climates of opinion, civilisations." The grandeur he beholds is "suddenly revealed as the mere superficies of a far vaster pattern in four dimensions," which is itself a foreshadowing of what lies beyond.

Martin Gardner, a polymath genius and engaging essayist who could write knowingly on most subjects ranging from string theory to G. K. Chesterton (and was a charming man to boot) concludes his collection *The Night Is Large* with an essay entitled "Surprise." He is defending his friend Georg Cantor against the charge of atheism, provoked by his transfinite set theory. Gardner knew him to be a deeply religious man "who placed God in a region that transcends all finite and infinite sets." Gardner continues, "it is because I, too, believe in this 'wholly other' realm, a realm in which our universe is an infinitesimal island, that I can call myself a mystic in the Platonic sense." He then goes on to explain Otto's concept of the 'holy'! Gardner died a Christian, believing in a God who is both transinfinite *and* come to earth incarnate: having it both ways, as Lewis put it.

Are these paradoxes? While reading they seem not to be. Only when ratiocination kicks in much later does puzzlement – not confusion, nor even doubt – but fogginess take hold. That, I believe, is because the great perspective that Lewis has provided dims, a perspective beyond anything elsewhere in his work, or (I would say) in Dante. And yet . . . "at the very zenith of complexity . . . a simplicity [there is Underhill] beyond all comprehension, ancient and young as spring, illimitable, pellucid, drew him with cords of infinite desire into its own stillness."

Is that, I wonder, the Unitive Way? "He went up into such quietness, a privacy, and a freshness that at the very moment when he stood farthest from our ordinary mode of being he had the sense of stripping off encumbrances and awaking from trance, and coming to himself." The Little End Room.

Even quoting at some length does not do justice to the Canticle of the Great Dance and its reliance upon the Ubiquitous Center. King Tor speaks, followed by Mars and then by others. Remember, often Ransom could not distinguish one speaker from the other:

> The Great Dance does not wait to be perfect. . . .
> We speak not of when it will begin. It has begun
> from before always. There was no time when we
> did not rejoice before His face as now. The dance
> which we dance is at the centre and for the dance
> all things were made. Blessed be He. . . . There is
> no way out of the centre save into the Bent Will
> which casts itself into the Nowhere. Blessed be
> He. . . . Thus each is equally at the centre. . . . All

that is made seems planless to the darkened mind, because there are more plans than are looked for. . . . Blessed be He.

That is when Ransom "thought he saw the Great Dance," woven from "intertwining undulations of many cords or bands of light, leaping over and under one another." Here the complexity is dazzling: "not all the cords were individuals: some were universal truths or universal qualities," so that "the movement grew yet swifter, the interweaving yet more ecstatic, the relevance of all to all yet more intense . . . and that part of him which could reason and remember was dropped farther and farther behind." After witnessing the Great Dance Ransom, experiences – "a simplicity beyond all comprehension."

So it is that *Perelandra* has hit, not the bottom but the roof of the firmament, Heaven itself – revealing a Reality no longer disputable. To be sure, the myth is not *itself* the Reality – no mystical vision is or can be – but *Perelandra* manages to arouse those "lineaments of ungratified desire." Who would not want to dive into the generosity, charity, and innocence; the commerce with animals and with spirits; and the delicious and willing sensual pleasures – each stimulating in us our own Joy? Who does not *hope* for that mountain top?

Perelandra, then, its own archetype, fresh and new, provided by neither an anthropologist nor a psychologist but by a mythmaker working in a genuinely mystical mode. David Downing gets it just right: as Ransom watches the Great Dance, "everything in the cosmos, from a momentary spark, to the lifespan of a star, shines out as a circle of swirling ribbons of interwoven light." We trust Ransom's report because Lewis does, because of what he says of him. So though we are at a remove – there are those watchful dragons, and Lewis's shyness – we are witnessing *Lewis's* mystical vision, a voluntary, if oblique, invasion of his own privacy.

Perelandra shows that we must fight fears both real and imagined, recognize a darkness and enter into combat with it, and then struggle to ascend, for in that ascent is escape from all those concentric worlds of self and culture and the like that would drag us down. Then, if we have persisted mightily to the heights, we might behold, not the end of the world but the beginning of an eternal glory.

Lewis, far from his "I never imagined," was *always* imagining, spiritually imagining, that is. He asks, "What will all . . . chatter and hearsay count (will you even be able to remember it?) when the anesthetic fog which we call 'nature' or 'the real world' [or 'culture'] fades away and the Presence in which you have always stood becomes palpable, immediate, and unavoidable?" *Narnia* and *Perelandra* invite us to see, suggesting what there is to *be* seen. But whether the other worlds are restrictive and dangerous, as are the Self, Culture, and Space-Time, or liberating, as are Imagination and Myth, finally we are warned against them or invited to pass through them to that final Other World.

The conclusion of *The Problem of Pain*, which I've cited earlier, merits full quotation:

> All the things that have ever deeply possessed your soul have been but . . . tantalising glimpses, promises never quite fulfilled. . . . But if it should really become manifest – if there ever came an echo that did not die away but swelled into the sound itself – you would know it. Beyond all possibility of doubt you would say 'Here at last is the thing I

was made for.'

–the *restored* Self speaking.

We will have moved through the concentric layers of patience and perseverance to Hope. For as we learn in 2 Cor 4:16-18 "this momentary light affliction is producing for us an eternal weight of glory" – a *weight of glory!* – "beyond all comparison, as we look not to what is seen but to what is unseen; for what is seen is transitory, but what is unseen is eternal."

Lewis used the word *Sehnsucht* to describe that feeling of want, a feeling attendant upon a realization that no particular thing, no matter how much we thought we really wanted it, can ever genuinely gratify a desire. It is a longing which brings pleasure, because all longing (no matter what the particular object) is for the same thing: God and heaven. Put another way, *Sehnsucht* is "spilled religion," and the drops may be full of blessing to the unconverted man who licks them and begins searching for the cup whence they spilled. Thus, the power of *Perelandra* to evince belief may derive from the fact that it offers a convincing portrayal of that Truth which, knowingly or not, we have always wanted.

This Reality and the longing it arouses exist permanently, independently, and unconditionally. That is why this utterly extra-literary phenomenon (what Lewis call the Dialectic of Desire), if "faithfully followed, would retrieve all mistakes, head you off from fake paths, and force you not to propound, but to live through, a sort of ontological proof." *Perelandra* provokes, provides us with, and is precisely that proof.

Somewhere Andre Dubus II, the (Catholic) short-story writer, has told of his problem with the sacraments as taught by the Catholic church. He has no difficulty accepting those seven; rather, he complains that there are *only* seven. The world itself, he argues, offers many more outward signs conveying grace than those seven, and they, too, come from Christ. Mystical writing can convey a similar grace. For many of us Lewis, above all in *Perelandra*, does exactly that. In Canto Twenty-five of the *Paradiso*, Dante proclaims (Esolen trans.),

> 'Hope,' said I, 'is the certain expectation
>> of future glory, and is born in us
>> by divine grace and merits we have won.
> This light has come to me from many stars,
>> but first was rained into my heart by him,
>> the sovereign singer of the sovereign Guide.
> 'Let them have hope in You who know Your name,'
>> he declares in his theody – and who
>> can fail to know His name, who shares my faith?

And with that Lewis has no argument: "I must keep alive in myself the desire for my true country, which I shall not find till after death: I must never let it get snowed under or turned aside; I must make it the main object of life to press on to that other country and to help others to do the same."

Dante ends his cosmic masterpiece with (Esolen trans.):

> That circle which appeared – in my poor style –
>> like a reflected radiance in Thee,
>> after my eyes had studied it awhile,
> Within, and in its own hue, seemed to be
>> tinted with the figure of a Man,
>> and so I gazed on it absorbedly
>
> . . . .

But mine were not the feathers for that flight,
> Save that the truth I longed for came to me,
> smiting my mind like lighting flashing
> bright.
Here ceased the powers of my high fantasy.

"Already," Dante continues, "were all my will and my desires turned . . . by the Love that moves the sun and the other stars."

Forty-five years before his death Lewis had written of having seen the glory; then when near that death he gazed fixedly ahead and said, *"Oh, I never imagined, I never imagined . . ."* To which I answer, "oh, yes, but you have." More than fifty years ago I read Jeffrey Hart's "The Re-birth of Christ" in *National Review* and since have read and studied almost all of Lewis there is to read. Having learned to say, "this, all of it, means me, or rather, "this *might* be me," I think, "really?"

Underhill writes, "When the greater love overwhelms the lesser, and your small self-consciousness is lost in the consciousness of the whole, it will be felt as an intense stillness, a quiet fruition of Reality." Such, she writes, "is a condition of *being* not of *seeing*." That comforts. *The Cloud of Unknowing* was written for those far beyond me but not, I believe, beyond Lewis.

Diogenes Allen (*Spiritual Theology: The Theology of Yesterday for Spiritual Help Today*) quotes Lewis's very dear friend, the Anglican theologian Austin Farrer (from his *Lord I Believe: Suggestions for Turning Creed Into Prayer*):

> There was a time when the lover of God . . . was putting together his knowledge of God. . . . But again, there was a time, not so soon reached but

> reached at last, when the knowledge of God
> gathered round the Name of God . . . [and] it was
> good, and indeed best of all, to be quiet at the place
> from which sprang all the paths of light and name
> the name of God, giving up the soul entirely to
> that unity of all perfection for which the Name had
> come to stand.

– in my case certainly aspirational: a hope I owe to Lewis, in whose company, in one way or another, I have spent the past fifty-five years, hearing his many voices, each a challenge and a comfort and a guide, to . . . ?

. . . what we fugitives have been seeking, where we hope to be, the only other world that matters, our No-So-Little End Room indeed (just through the stable door). At the end of the day what we owe to Lewis is this: he made a path – keep looking, and you will find yours somewhere in his work – he is saying, as the good apostle does, "follow me." We cannot get to Narnia, but we can get to the peak of that mountain, to the very edge of the eschaton. What irony for the fugitive, to find that *being caught and getting home are the same.*

Rather than playing at so many interior parallel lives as though Plutarch wrote me, and spectating, not quite believing that I am part of the plan of the grandeur of hope and eternity that Lewis has shown me, I should have known that Lewis has indeed been speaking to me all along and so I should have been praying:

> Having plied among your several Selves,
> Legionnaire, choose one.
> A sorry ploy is this 'Integration.'

Hell is the play of intellection.

Now: choose the One.

Finally Tor and Tinidril and Ransom, whom Tor calls "'friend and saviour," bid farewell to him, as Tor prays, 'Speak of us always to Maleldil as we speak always of you. The splendour, the love, and the strength be upon you.'"

> Then came the great cumbrous noise of the lid being fastened on above him. Then, for a few seconds, noises without, in the world from which he was eternally divided. Then his consciousness was engulfed,

leaving behind a vision about which *we* say, "I never imagined, I never imagined," but about which I say, we did not have to. Our mystic did it for us.

Postscript

Following upon a chapter called Strife, this one is called Awe. The former brings us to a great depth, this one to a very great height which I claim is, in fact, the peak of Lewis's apologetic project – a great vision of Hope at the core of Lewis's Christian work. It is also at the core of spiritual theology; that is, the development to perfection of every soul. That is the acre that Lewis plowed, in his own life and in his work, especially through his great hero (and mine) Elwin Ransom. Therein lies Lewis's great achievement: the breadth and depth of his influence.

But there is also his impact on many millions of individual readers. Perhaps one example will demonstrate what I mean. In 1974, Alexandra, my nearly three-year-old son Jim and I traveled to Oxford for my one-semester sabbatical. On our behalf Walter Hooper had rented an upstairs apartment at 286 Iffley Road. I would write a short article called "A Clerke of Oxenforde" (the title cribbed from Chaucer) for the fifth anniversary issue of the New York C. S. Lewis Society Bulletin. In it I provided a verbal tour of places that mattered to Lewis, such as the first room he stayed in and (of course) The Eagle and Child, where the Inklings would meet.

But at the same time I was studying *A Grief Observed*, purported to be a contemporary diary that Lewis kept after the death of his wife Joy. It is a psychological and spiritual cartography of grief. In it the author (Lewis published it pseudonymously) is bereft, then in despair (though never quite to the point of not believing in God), then is hopeful. My argument was (and remains) that the book is, in part, a contrivance. It is not in whole the contemporary diary it seems to be. (One need only read Lewis's Five Sonnets, written nearly ten years earlier, to see the literary source of much of the book.)

I was pleased with my contention, not least because it is (or was) contentious. Moreover, I was delighted to be able to say that Lewis would marshal even such a cataclysmic personal loss for the apologetic purpose of counseling from a Christian perspective others who had suffered similarly. I, too, he was saying, have traveled that road to the depths, but, though it is a horror, it does rise eventually. Now in the middle of this pondering we gave a dinner for Walter, his mother, and her sister (Walter's Aunt Twiggy). The two ladies were visiting from North Carolina, where Walter had been born. The phone rang just as we sat down.

My brother was calling to tell me that our father had

died hours earlier from a massive heart attack. He was fifty-four. When I hung up I saw that Alexandra and our guests, who had inferred the news, could only stare. As for me, I had lost my best friend and went to pieces. After gathering myself, we dined (sort of), and the next day Alexandra made plans for my trip to New York for the funeral. I was heartened by the assurance that I was leaving my family in the very best of hands. In New York I was comforted by the many people who came, both to the wake and the funeral, and by what they said to me about a man whom I knew as the most congenial and thoughtful who had walked the earth.

Here is my point. When I got back to my Oxford desk and thought to pick up where I had left off, *I found I was dealing with a completely different book.* Contrivance or not, it rang absolutely true – as I would experience over the next year – in its every word. It was not only a comfort, not only that but a companion. With Alexandra (who loved my father and was herself grieving but did not let it show) and C. S. Lewis as a guide, right there at my shoulder, I staggered through.

Nearly two hundred pages earlier, I wrote what now I repeat. Here, too, is Lewis's achievement: one, and one, and one – one reader at a time.

SELECTED BIBLIOGRAPHY

Adey, Lionel. *C. S. Lewis's 'Great War' with Owen Barfield.* University of Victoria, *English Literary Studies* (No. 4), 1978.

_____. *C. S. Lewis: Writer, Dreamer & Mentor.* Grand Rapids: Wm. B. Eerdmans, 1998.

Allen, Diogenes. *Spiritual Theology: The Theology of Yesterday for Spiritual Help Today.* New York: Cowley Publications, 1997.

Altschul, Sol, ed. *Childhood Bereavement and Its Aftermath.* Emotions and Behavior Monographs: Monograph No. 8. Madison, Conn.: International Universities Press, Inc., 1988.

Bevan, Edwyn. *Symbolism and Belief* (1938). Boston: Beacon Press, 1957.

Booth, Wayne. *The Rhetoric of Fiction*, 2nd ed. Chicago: The University of Chicago Press, 1983.

Chesterton, G. K. *The Everlasting Man.* New York: Dodd, Mead & Company, 1925.

Como, James. *Branches to Heaven: the Geniuses of C. S. Lewis.* Dallas: Spence Publishing Company, 1998.

_____. *C. S. Lewis: A Very Short Introduction.* Oxford: Oxford University Press, 2019.

_____. *Remembering C. S. Lewis* (3rd ed. of *C. S. Lewis at the Breakfast Table*). San Francisco: Ignatius Press, 2005.

Dante. *Purgatory.* Trans. Anthony Esolen. New York: The Modern Library, 2003.

_____. *Paradise*. Trans. Anthony Esolen. New York: The Modern Library, 2004.

Downing, David. *Into the Region of Awe: Mysticism in C. S. Lewis*. Downers Grove: InterVarsity Press, 2002.

_____. *Planets in Peril: A Critical Study of C. S. Lewis's Ransom Trilogy*. Amherst: The University of Massachusetts Press, 1992.

Frazer, Sir James George. *The Golden Bough: A Study in Magic and Religion*. New York: The Macmillan Company (one volumeabridged edition), 1963.

Goetz, Stewart. *A Philosophical Walking Tour with C. S. Lewis (Why It Did Not Include Rome)* New York: Bloomsbury Academic, 2014.

Hannay, Margaret Patterson. *C. S. Lewis*. New York: Frederick Ungar Publishing Company, 1981.

Harris, Maxine. *The Loss That Is Forever*. New York: Penguin Books, 1996.

Holmer, Paul. *C. S. Lewis: The Shape of His Faith and Thought*. New York: Harper & Row, 1976.

Howard, Thomas. *C. S. Lewis: A Reading of His Fiction*. San Francisco: Ignatius Press, 1987.

Jung, Carl Gustav. *Mysterium Coniunctionis*. New York: Pantheon Books, 1963.

_____. *Psychological Reflections*, ed. Yolanda Jacobi. New York: Princeton University Press, 1953.

_____. *Psychology and Religion*. New Haven: Yale University Press's, 1938.

_____. *The Spirit in Man, Art, and Literature.* New York: Routledge, 1966.

Keegan, John. *The Face of Battle.* New York: Barnes & Noble Books, 1993.

Langrish, Katherine. *From Spare Oom to War Drobe: Travels in Narnia with My Nine-Year-Old Self.* London: Darton, Longman and Todd Ltd., 2021.

Lawlor. John. *C. S. Lewis: Memories and Reflections.* Dallas, Spence Publishing Company,1998.

Lewis, C. S. *An Experiment in Criticism.* Cambridge: The University Press, 1961.

_____. *Collected Letters.* Vols. I-III ed. Walter Hooper.   London: Harper Collins, 2000, 2004, 2006.

_____. *Essay Collections* (2vols). Ed. Lesley Walmsley. London: Harper Collins, 2000.

_____. *Narrative Poems.* Ed. Walter Hooper. London: Geoffrey Bles, 1969.

_____. *Out of the Silent Planet.* New York: The Macmillan Company, 1968.

_____. *Poems.* Ed. Walter Hooper. London: Fount Paperbacks, 1994.

_____. *Perelandra.* New York: The Macmillan Company, 1968.

_____. *Surprised by Joy.* New York: Harcourt, Brace & World, Inc., 1955.

_____. *The Discarded Image.* London: The Cambridge Univesity Press, 1964.

_____. *The Pilgrim's Regress*. Grand Rapids: Wm. B. Eerdmans, 1992.

_____. *Till We Have Faces*. Grand Rapids: Wm. B Eerdmans, 1956.

_____. *The Voyage of the 'Dawn Treader'*. Harmondsworth: Puffin Books, 1967.

Manlove, Colin. *C. S. Lewis: His Literary Achievement*. Cheshire, CT: Winged Lion Press, 2010.

Miller, Laura. *The Magician's Book: A Skeptics Adventures in Narnia*. New York: Back Bay, 2008.

Murphy, James J. "St. Augustine and the Debate About a Christian Rhetoric" *Quarterly Journal of Speech* 46 (1960): 400-410.

Newman, John Henry. *An Essay in Aid of a Grammar of Assent* (1870; 8th ed. 1889). Ed. I. T. Ker. Oxford: Clarendon Press, 1985.

Otto Rudolph. *The Idea of the Holy: an inquiry into the non-rational factor in the idea of the divine and its relation to the rational* (1917). Trans. John W. Harvey, 2nd ed. New York: Oxford University Press, 1958.

Percy, Walker. *The Message in the Bottle: How Queer Man Is, How Queer Language Is, and What One Has to Do with the Other*. New York: Farrar, Straus and Giroux, 1984.

Poe, Harry Lee. *Becoming C. S. Lewis: A Biography of Young Jack Lewis (1898-1918)*. Wheaton: Crossway, 2019.

_____. *The Making of C. S. Lewis: From Atheist to Apologist (1918-1945)*. Wheaton: Crossway, 2021.

Raphael, Beverly. "The Young Child and the Death of a Parent." *The Place of Achievement in Human Behavior.* Ed. Colin Murray Parkes and Joan Stevenson-Hinde. New York: Basic Books, 131-150.

Richards, I. A. *Practical Criticism.* New York: Harcourt, Brace & World, Inc., 1929.

Sahler, Olle Jane Z., ed. *The Child and Death.* St. Louis: The C. V. Mossby Co., 1978.

Sammons, Martha C. *A Guide Through C. S. Lewis' Space Trilogy.* Westchester, Ill.: Cornestone, 1980.

Schwartz, Sandford. *C. S. Lewis on the Final Frontier: Science and the Supernatural in the Space Trilogy.* New York: Oxford University Press, 2009.

Tanquerey, Adolphe. *The Spiritual Life: A Treatise on Ascetical and Mystical Theology,* trans. Herman Branderis (1930). 2nd and revised edition, Charlotte: TAN Books, 2000.

Underhill, Evelyn. *Mysticism.* London: Methuen, 1911.

Walsh, Chad. *The Literary Legacy of C. S. Lewis.* New York: Harcourt Brace Jovanovich, 1979.

White, William Luther. *The Image of Man in C. S. Lewis.* Nashville: Abingdon Press, 1969.

Wright, Marjorie Evelyn. "The Vision of Cosmic Order in the Oxford Mythmakers." *Imagination and the Spirit.* Ed. Charles Huttar. Grand Rapids: Wm. B. Eerdmans, 1971. Pp. 259-276.

Spiritual Writers

Augustine of Hippo, *Confessions*

Bernard of Clairvaux, *The Twelve Steps of Humility and Pride* and *On Loving God*

Boehme, Jacob. *The Way to Christ*

Bonaventure, *Journey of the Mind to God*, *The Triple Way, or, Love Enkindled*, *The Mystical Vine*, *On the Perfection of Life*

Catherine of Sienna, *The Dialogue of St. Catherine of Sienna*

The Cloud of Unknowing (anon.)

Francis de Sales, *Introduction to the Devout and Holy Life*

Hildegard of Bingen, *Mystical Revelations from Jesus Christ*

Hilton, Walter, *The Scale of Perfection*

John of the Cross, *Poems of St. John of The Cross*

Dame Julian of Norwich, *Revelations of Divine Love*

Law, William, *A Serious Call to a Devout and Holy Life*

Teresa of Avila, *The Interior Castle*, *The Way of Perfection*, and *The Life of Saint Teresa of Avila by Herself*

Theologica Germanica (anon.)

Thomas à Kempis, *The Imitation of Christ*

Traherne, Thomas, *Centuries of Meditation*

OTHER BOOKS FROM WINGED LION PRESS

C. S. LEWIS

No Ordinary People:
Twenty-one Friendships of C.S. Lewis
Joel Heck

The creator of the internet database Chronologically Lewis explores 21 friendships, some close and others casual, providing a look into the private life of one of the twentieth century's most engaging and e ective writers. The book title comes from his famous sermon "The Weight of Glory"..

The Leadership of C. S. Lewis:
Ten Traits to Encourage Change & Growth
Crystal Hurd

This book is for readers interested in developing leadership traits by examining how C. S. Lewis became such an influential spiritual leader for our times. The chapters include: Humility, Morality, Vision, Courage, Intellect, Compassion, Duty, Inspiration, Resilience, and Creativity.

C. S. Lewis: Views From Wake Forest:
Essays on C. S. Lewis
Michael Travers, editor

Contains sixteen scholarly presentations from the international C. S. Lewis convention in Wake Forest, NC. Walter Hooper shares his important essay "Editing C. S. Lewis," a chronicle of publishing decisions after Lewis' death in 1963.

> *"Scholars from a variety of disciplines address a wide*
> *range of issues. The happy result is a fresh and expansive*
> *view of an author who well deserves this kind of*
> *thoughtful attention."*
> Diana Pavlac Glyer, author of *The Company They Keep*

The Hidden Story of Narnia:
A Book-By-Book Guide to Lewis' Spiritual Themes
Will Vaus

A book of insightful commentary equally suited for teens or adults – Will Vaus points out connections between the *Narnia* books and spiritual/biblical themes, as well as between ideas in the *Narnia* books and C. S. Lewis' other books. Learn what Lewis himself said about the overarching and unifying thematic structure of the Narnia books. That is what this book explores; what C. S. Lewis called "the hidden story" of Narnia. Each chapter includes questions for individual use or small group discussion.

Why I Believe in Narnia:
33 Reviews and Essays on the Life and Work of C. S. Lewis
James Como

Chapters range from reviews of critical books, documentaries and movies to evaluations of Lewis' books to biographical analysis.

> *"A valuable, wide-ranging collection of essays by one of the best informed and most accute commentators on Lewis' work and ideas."*
> Peter Schakel, author of *Imagination & the Arts in C. S. Lewis*

C. S. Lewis: His Literary Achievement
Colin Manlove

> *"This is a positively brilliant book, written with splendor, elegance, profundity and evidencing an enormous amount of learning. This is probably not a book to give a first-time reader of Lewis. But for those who are more broadly read in the Lewis corpus this book is an absolute gold mine of information. The author gives us a magnificent overview of Lewis' many writings, tracing for us thoughts and ideas which recur throughout, and at the same time telling us how each book differs from the others. I think it is not extravagant to call C. S. Lewis: His Literary Achievement a tour de force."*
> Robert Merchant, *St. Austin Review*, Book Review Editor

In the Footsteps of C. S. Lewis:
A Photographic Pilgrimage to the British Isles
Will Vaus

Over the course of thirty years, Will Vaus has journeyed
to the British Isles many times to walk in the footsteps of
C. S. Lewis. His private photographs of the significant
places in Lewis' life have captured the imagination of
audiences in the US and UK to whom he has lectured on
the Oxford don and his work. This, in turn, prompted
the idea of this collection of 78 full-color photographs,
interwoven with details about Lewis' life and work. The
combination of words and pictures make this a wonderful
addition to the library of all Lewis scholars and readers.

Speaking of Jack: A C. S. Lewis Discussion Guide
Will Vaus

Included here are introductions to most of Lewis' books as
well as questions designed to stimulate discussion about
Lewis' life and work. These materials have been "road-
tested" with real groups made up of young and old, some
very familiar with Lewis and some newcomers. *Speaking
of Jack* may be used in an existing book discussion group,
to start a C. S. Lewis Society, or as a guide to your own
exploration of Lewis' books.

Light: C. S. Lewis's First and Final Short Story
Charlie W. Starr
Foreword by Walter Hooper

Charlie Starr explores the questions surrounding the
"Light" manuscript, a later version of story titled "A Man
Born Blind." The insights into this story provide a new key
to understanding some of Lewis's most profound ideas.

> *"As literary journalism, both investigative and critical, it
> is top shelf"*
> James Como, author of *Remembering C. S. Lewis*

> *"Starr shines a new and illuninating light on one of
> Lewis's most intriguing stories"*
> Michael Ward, author of *Planet Narnia*

C. S. Lewis & Philosophy as a Way of Life: His Philosophical Thoughts
Adam Barkman

C. S. Lewis is rarely thought of as a "philosopher" per se despite having both studied and taught philosophy for several years at Oxford. Lewis's long journey to Christianity was essentially philosophical – passing through seven different stages. This 624 page book is an invaluable reference for C. S. Lewis scholars and fans alike

C. S. Lewis' Top Ten: Influential Books and Authors, Volume One
Will Vaus

Based on his books, marginal notes, and personal letters, Will Vaus explores Lewis' reading of the ten books he said shaped his vocational attitude and philosophy of life. Volume One covers the first three authors/books: George MacDonald: *Phantastes*, G.K. Chesterton: *The Everlasting Man*, and Virgil: *The Aneid*. Vaus offers a brief biography of each author with a helpful summary of their books.

> *"Thorough, comprehensive, and illuminating"*
> Rolland Hein, Author of *George MacDonald: Victorian Mythmaker*

C. S. Lewis' Top Ten: Influential Books and Authors, Volume Two
Will Vaus

Volume Two covers the following authors/books: George Herbert: *The Temple*, William Wordsworth: *The Prelude*, Rudopf Otto, *The Idea of the Holy*.

C. S. Lewis' Top Ten: Influential Books and Authors, Volume Three
Will Vaus

Volume Three covers the following authors/books: Boethius: *The Consolation of Philosophy*, James Boswell, *The Life of Samuel Johnson*, Charles Williams: *Descent into Hell*, A.J. Balfour: *Thiesm and Humanism*.

C. S. Lewis Goes to Heaven:
A Reader's Guide to The Great Divorce
David G. Clark

This is the first book devoted solely to this often neglected book and the first to reveal several important secrets Lewis concealed within the story. Lewis felt his imaginary trip to Hell and Heaven was far better than his book *The Screwtape Letters*, which has become a classic. Readers will discover the many literary and biblical influences Lewis utilized in writing his brilliant novel.

C. S. Lewis Goes to Hell
A Companion and Study Guide to The Screwtape Letters
William O'Flaherty

The creator and host of "All About Jack" has written a guide to *The Screwtape Letters* suitable for groups or individuals, featuring an index of themes, summaries of each letter, questions for reflection, and over a half-dozen appendices of useful information.

Joy and Poetic Imagination: Understanding C. S. Lewis's "Great War" with Owen Barfield and its Significance for Lewis's Conversion and Writings
Stephen Thorson

Author Stephen Thorson began writing this book over 30 years ago and published parts of it in articles during Barfield's lifetime. Barfield wrote to Thorson in 1983 saying, ""*...you have surveyed the divergence between Lewis and myself very fairly, and truly 'in depth...*'". This book explains the "Great War" between these two friends.

Mythopoeic Narnia: Memory, Metaphor, and Metamorphoses in C. S. Lewis's The Chronicles of Narnia
Salwa Khoddam

Dr. Khoddam offers a fresh approach to the *Narnia* books based on an inquiry into Lewis' readings and use of classical and Christian symbols. She explores the literary and intellectual contexts of these stories, the traditional myths and motifs, and places them in the company of the greatest Christian mythopoeic works of Western Literature.

Exploring the Eternal Goodness: Selected Writings of David L. Neuhouser
Joe Ricke and Lisa Ritchie, Editors

In 1997, due to David's perseverance, the Brown Collection of books by and about C. S. Lewis and related authors came to Taylor University and the Lewis and Friends Colloquium began. This book of selected writings reflects his scholarship in math and literature, as well as his musings on beauty and the imagination. The twenty-one tributes are an indication of the many lives he has influenced. This book is meant to acknowledge David L. Neuhouser for his contributions to scholarship and to honor his life of friendship, encouragement, and genuine goodness.

Inklings Forever, Volume X: Proceedings from the 10th Francis White Ewbank Colloquiunm on C. S. Lewis & Friends
Joe Ricke and Rick Hill, Editors

In June 2016, the 10th biennial Frances Ewbank Colloquium on C. S. Lewis and Friends convened at Taylor University with the special theme of "friendship." Many of the essays and creative pieces collected in this book explore the important relationships of Inklings-related authors, as well as the relationships between those authors and other, sometimes rather surprising, "friends." The year 2016 marked the 90th anniversary of the first meeting of C. S. Lewis and J.R.R. Tolkien – a creative friendship of epic proportions

> *What a feast! It is rare that a book of proceedings captures the energy and spirit of the conference itself: this one does. I recommend it.*
> Diana Pavlac Glyer, Professor of English at Azusa Pacific University and author of *The Company They Keep* and *Bandersnatch: C. S. Lewis, J. R. R. Tolkien, and the Creative Collaboration of the Inklings*

The Faithful Imagination: Papers from the 2018 Francis White Ewbank Colloquiunm on C. S. Lewis & Friends
Joe Ricke and Ashley Chu, Editors

Sunbeams and Bottles:
The Theology, Thought, and Reading of C.S. Lewis
James Prothero

C.S. Lewis once said of Christ that he was the most elusive of teachers and that trying to systematize the Lord's teaching was like trying to bottle sunbeams. *Sunbeams and Bottles* is not only a response to attempts in the last decade to tie Lewis to particular political and social agendas, but it is also a fresh look at his thought in light of his reading. The author posits that Lewis really was a theologian in spite of his protests against the idea.

CHRISTIAN LIVING

Keys to Growth: Meditations on the Acts of the Apostles
Will Vaus

Every living thing or person requires certain ingredients in order to grow, and if a thing or person is not growing, it is dying. *The Acts of the Apostles* is a book that is all about growth. Will Vaus has been meditating and preaching on *Acts* for the past 30 years. In this volume, he offers the reader forty-one keys from the entire book of Acts to unlock spiritual growth in everyday life.

Open Before Christmas: Devotional Thoughts For The Holiday Season
Will Vaus

Author Will Vaus seeks to deepen the reader's knowledge of Advent and Christmas leading up to Epiphany. Readers are provided with devotional thoughts for each day that help them to experience this part of the Church Year in a spiritually enriching way.

God's Love Letter: Reflections on I John
Will Vaus

Various words for "love" appear thirty-five times in the five brief chapters of I John. This book invites you on a journey of reading and reflection: reading this book in the New Testament and reflecting on God's love for us, our love for God, and our love for one another.

Jogging with G.K. Chsterton: 65 Earthshaking Expeditions
Robert Moore-Jumonville

Jogging with G.K. Chesterton is a showcase for the merry mind of Chesterton. But Chesterton's lighthearted wit always runs side-by-side with his weighty wisdom. These 65 "earthshaking expeditions" will keep you smiling and thinking from start to finish. *"This is a delightfully improbable book in which Chesterton puts us through our spiritual and intellectual exercises."*

Joseph Pearce, author of *Wisdom and Innocence: A Life of G.K. Chesterton*

GEORGE MACDONALD

Phantastes by George MacDonald: Annotated Edition
John Pennington and Roderick McGillis, Editors

Phantastes was a groundbreaking book in 1858 and continues to be a seminal example of great fantasy literature. Its elusive meaning is both alluring and perplexing, inviting readers to experience a range of deep feelings and a sense of profound truth. This annotated edition, by two renowned MacDonald scholars, provides a wealth of information to better understand and enjoy this masterpiece.

Crossing a Great Frontier:
Essays on George MacDonald's Phantastes
John Pennington, Editor

> *"This is the first collection of scholarly essays on George MacDonald's seminal romance Phantastes. Appropriately to the age of its hero Anodos, here we have twenty-one of the best essays written on Phantastes from 1972 onwards, in which straightforward literary analysis works together with contextual, psychological, metaphysical, alchemical and scientific approaches to the elucidation of this moving and elusive work."*
> Colin Manlove, author of *Scotland's Forgotten Treasure: The Visionary Novels of George MacDonald*

Lilith by George MacDonald:
Annotated Scholarly Edition
John Pennington & Roderick McGillis, Editors
Following the acclaim of their scholarly edition of MacDonald's *Phantastes*, these editors combine their expertise to create a foundational resource to enjoy *Lilith*, a masterpiece of fantasy literature. Over 500 footnotes, seven appendices, reviews, and more.

Behind the Back of the North Wind:
Essays on George MacDonald's Classic Book
Edited and with Introduction by John Pennington and Roderick McGillis

The unique blend of fairy tale atmosphere and social realism in this novel laid the groundwork for modern fantasy literature. Sixteen essays by various authors are accompanied by an instructive introduction, extensive index, and beautiful illustrations.

Diary of an Old Soul & The White Page Poems
George MacDonald and Betty Aberlin

The first edition of George MacDonald's book of daily poems included a blank page opposite each page of poems. Readers were invited to write their own reflections on the "white page." Betty Aberlin responded to MacDonald's invitation with daily poems of her own.

> *Betty Aberlin's close readings of George MacDonald's verses and her thoughtful responses to them speak clearly of her poetic gifts and spiritual intelligence*
> Luci Shaw, poet

George MacDonald: Literary Heritage and Heirs
Roderick McGillis, editor

This latest collection of 14 essays sets a new standard that will influence MacDonald studies for many more years. George MacDonald experts are increasingly evaluating his entire corpus within the nineteenth century context.

> *This comprehensive collection represents the best of contemporary scholarship on George MacDonald.*
> Rolland Hein, author of *George MacDonald: Victorian Mythmaker*

In the Near Loss of Everything: George MacDonald's Son in America
Dale Wayne Slusser

In the summer of 1887, George MacDonald's son Ronald, newly engaged to artist Louise Blandy, sailed from England to America to teach school. The next summer he returned to England to marry Louise and bring her back to America. On August 27, 1890, Louise died leaving him with an infant daughter. Ronald once described losing a beloved spouse as "the near loss of everything". Dale Wayne Slusser unfolds this poignant story with unpublished letters and photos that give readers a glimpse into the close-knit MacDonald family. Also included is Ronald's essay about his father, *George MacDonald: A Personal Note*, plus a selection from Ronald's 1922 fable, *The Laughing Elf*, about the necessity of both sorrow and joy in life.

160

A Novel Pulpit: Sermons From George MacDonald's Fiction
David L. Neuhouser

Each of the sermons has an introduction giving some explanation of the setting of the sermon or of the plot. *"MacDonald's novels are both stimulating and thought-provoking. This collection of sermons from ten novels serve to bring out the 'freshness and brilliance' of MacDonald's message."from the author's introduction*

Through the Year with George MacDonald: 366 Daily Readings
Rolland Hein, editor

These page-length excerpts from sermons, novels and letters are given an appropriate theme/heading and a complementary Scripture passage for daily reading. An inspiring introduction to the artistic soul and Christian vision of George MacDonald.

Shadows and Chivalry: C. S. Lewis and George MacDonald on Suffering, Evil, and Death
Jeff McInnis

Shadows and Chivalry studies the influence of George MacDonald upon one of the most influential writers of modern times, C. S. Lewis—the creator of Narnia, literary critic, and best-selling apologist. Without ever ceasing to be a story of one man's influence upon another, the study also serves as an exploration of each writer's thought on, and literary visions of, good and evil.

The Downstretched Hand: Individual Development in MacDonald's Major Fantasies for Children
Lesley Willis Smith

Smith demonstrates that MacDonald is fully aware of the need to integrate the unconscious into the conscious in order to achieve mature individuation. However, for MacDonald, true maturity and fulfillment can only be gained through a relationship with God. By exploring MacDonald's major biblical themes into his own myth, Smith reveals his literary genius and profound understanding of the human psyche. Smith interacts with other leading scholarship and in the context of other works by MacDonald.

BIOGRAPHY

Sheldon Vanauken:
The Man Who Received "A Severe Mercy"
Will Vaus

In this biography we discover: Vanauken the struggling student, the bon-vivant lover, the sailor who witnessed the bombing of Pearl Harbor, the seeker who returned to faith through C. S. Lewis, the beloved professor of English literature and history, the feminist and anti-war activist who participated in the March on the Pentagon, the bestselling author, and Vanauken the convert to Catholicism. What emerges is the portrait of a man relentlessly in search of beauty, love, and truth, a man who believed that, in the end, he found all three.

> *"This is a charming biography about a doubly charming man who wrote a triply charming book. It is a great way to meet the man behind A Severe Mercy."*
> Peter Kreeft, author of *Jacob's Ladder: 10 Steps to Truth*

Remembering Roy Campbell:
The Memoirs of his Daughters, Anna and Tess
Introduction by Judith Lütge Coullie, Editor
Preface by Joseph Pearce

Anna and Teresa Campbell were the daughters of the handsome young South African poet and writer, Roy Campbell (1901-1957), and his beautiful English wife, Mary Garman. In their frank and moving memoirs, Anna and Tess recall the extraordinary, and often very difficult, lives they shared with their exceptional parents. Over 50 photos, 344 footnotes, timeline of Campbell's life, and complete index.

POETS AND POETRY

In the Eye of the Beholder:
How to See the World Like a Romantic Poet
Louis Markos

Born out of the French Revolution and its radical faith that a nation could be shaped and altered by the dreams and visions of its people, British Romantic Poetry was founded on a belief that the objects and realities of our world, whether natural or human, are not fixed in stone but can be molded and transformed by the visionary eye of the poet. A separate bibliographical essay is provided for readers listing accessible biographies of each poet and critical studies of their work.

The Cat on the Catamaran:
A Christmas Tale
John Martin

Here is a modern-day parable of a modern-day cat with modern-day attitudes. Riverboat Dan is a "cool" cat on a perpetual vacation from responsibility. He's *The Cat on the Catamaran* – sailing down the river of life. Dan keeps his guilty conscience from interfering with his fun until he runs into trouble. But will he have the courage to believe that it's never too late to change course? (For ages 10 to adult)

> *"This book is a joy, and as companionable as a good-natured cat."*
> Walter Hooper, author of *C.S. Lewis: Companion and Guide*

Made in the USA
Middletown, DE
06 February 2023

24118185R00104